broken promises, mended hearts

maintaining trust in love relationships

JOEL D. BLOCK, PH.D.

Contemporary Books

Chicago New York San Francisco Lisbon London Madrid Mexico City
Milan New Delhi San Juan Seoul Singapore Sydney Toronto

Library of Congress Cataloging-in-Publication Data

Block, Joel D.
    Broken promises, mended hearts : maintaining trust in love relationships /
Joel D. Block
        p.   cm.
    Includes bibliographical references and index.
    ISBN 0-8092-2396-1 (hardcover) 0-8092-2398-8 (paperback)
    1. Trust.   2. Love.   3. Man-woman relationships.   4. Couples.   I. Title.

    BF575. T7 B56   2000
    306.7—dc21   00-22723

    4 5 6 7 8 9 10 11 12   AGM/AGM   3 2 1 0 9 8 7 6 5 4

ISBN 0-8092-2396-1 (hardcover)
ISBN 0-8092-2398-8 (paperback)

McGraw-Hill books are available at special quantity discounts to use as premiums and sales promotions, or for use in corporate training programs. For more information, please write to the Director of Special Sales, Professional Publishing, McGraw-Hill, Two Penn Plaza, New York, NY 10121-2298. Or contact your local bookstore.

This book is printed on acid-free paper.

To Gail, who has earned my absolute trust

CONTENTS

AUTHOR'S NOTE

The identities of people described in this book were protected by altering names and other external characteristics, but the basic psychological and social dynamics involved have been preserved. Any resemblance to real persons is strictly intended; any precise identification with real persons is, I trust, impossible.

Some of the terms used throughout the book require clarification. The terms *wife, husband, spouse, partner, love partner, relationship,* and *marriage,* are used interchangeably with the intention of including all couples, married or not. In no instance are these terms meant to exclude anyone. For the trust issues that I address are fundamental. They are faced by all couples. I have thought it best to give examples only on the basis of my own professional experience, which has been primarily with male-female couples. Yet it is my hope that this book will prove helpful to any two people engaged in an ongoing love relationship of any type.

The Bridge Connecting Us

Trust is like a bridge between individuals that enables us to cross over to each other. Whether as friends, business associates, or lovers, we feel safe and secure with a strong foundation beneath us. In love relationships in particular, we feel safe enough to express love and attain intimacy when the bridge is solid and we feel confident of its support.

Trust is defined as the assured reliance on the character, strength, or truth of someone or something. More immediately applicable to love relations is the verb "to trust": to have faith or confidence that something is or will be as expected. Those couples who enjoy trust, who give trust to each other, are among the most fortunate people.

When trust is undermined and we feel disappointed or betrayed, such as when we are deceived by a lie or exploited by a broken promise, we pull back just as we would on a bridge that has become unsteady. Our expectations are shattered. Trust in our own judgment is undermined. We feel a sense of loss that a loved one didn't respect us enough to be honest with us or fulfill his or her promise to us. In short, we feel violated and diminished, because trust has been broken. It is a weakened bridge that we can no longer cross, leaving us scrambling to get back to the safety of solid ground.

At times we may believe incorrectly that our trust has been violated. Acting accordingly may result in what we really fear, the loss of love. Our own self-created mistrust can lead us to avoid the bridge, or weaken it until it collapses.

The more important the relationship, the more we feel betrayed and devastated by the result of a loss of trust. Mistrust contains its own seeds for further destruction.

Love, Mistrust, and Loss

Consider the story of Robert and Jean—a classic example of love, mistrust, and loss. Robert, a thirty-nine-year-old electrical engineer, had been happily married to Jean, an editor of a popular weekly magazine in the Boston area. He had met Jean when both were attending Harvard. It took Robert several years to feel really sure of their relationship. Since he had grown up being more comfortable with objects than people, he felt more in control solving complex engineering problems than having close relationships. He also felt wary about crossing the bridge and allowing himself to love, because his parents had gone through a bitter divorce when he was a child. Thus, it took him a long time to warm up and trust others. After only occasionally dating other women, he experienced a strong attraction to Jean. Finally, after three years of exclusive dating, he felt ready to make a lifelong commitment to her.

For the first few months of marriage, everything was fine. Then Robert's company assigned him to a major international project that required extensive travel. As a result, he and Jean were separated for weeks at a time. Still, Robert remained completely loyal and never considered even looking at another woman. He was certain that Jean felt the same way, since he trusted her so deeply. He was reassured because they shared the same values, and when he did return home for brief periods during his travels, she seemed so adoring and responsive. Nothing seemed to have changed.

However, after one of his trips, Robert went with Jean to a party that changed everything. After a few hours, he began experiencing the effects of jet lag and headed upstairs to a bedroom to lie down for a few minutes. When he swung the bedroom door open, he was surprised to see Jean standing there talking to Walt, a friend he had known since college. As he perceived it, Jean and Walt were standing quite close to each other having a serious conversation; when Jean looked up as he entered, her face flushed and her body seemed to jerk nervously.

Immediately he thought the two must be on "intimate terms." But not wanting to provoke a confrontation, he found another room to lie down in. At home, when he asked Jean about the conversation, she denied that anything was wrong. "We were just talking and I was startled to see you," she said.

After this incident, however, based on what he perceived and believed, Robert's trust in Jean had been fatally pierced. He had always valued safety, security, and predictability, and now he felt uncertain about Jean's love, despite her denials. He was so unnerved that he rejected a few friends' unsolicited advice to consider the incident innocent and get on with his life. Instead, he felt angered by their advice, convinced of Jean's betrayal.

Based on this view, he began to close down emotionally. He talked to Jean less, and they became increasingly distant, destroying the intimacy they once shared. At the same time, Robert began to look for examples of deception and betrayal by Jean to support his view. For example, he started to regard minor mistakes or discrepancies as deceptions, such as when the credit card reports showed that Jean spent more money on something than she said she did or when she arrived home later than she said she would. Meanwhile, Robert engaged in actions that further shut Jean out of his life, damaging what was left of the bridge between them, such as retreating into his work or going directly from work into his garage to restore an antique car.

Not surprisingly, Jean soon began to retreat as well, into her own work and outside activities. Their discussions, when they did happen to see each other at home, were mostly mundane, involving the weather or problems in making travel connections in the city. Occasionally they argued, such as when Jean complained that Robert was being too judgmental and unfairly scrutinizing her activities.

Needless to say, their relationship ended up in divorce court. After the divorce Robert discovered that Walt and Jean had indeed been lovers but *had not been* at the time Robert walked in on them. In a confrontation with Walt after the breakup of the marriage, Robert learned that Walt and Jean had only been talking that evening at the party; Jean's denial had been truthful. But several months after the incident she ran into Walt on the street and, feeling shut out by Robert's growing withdrawal, Jean confided to her friend her desperate loneliness, and *that* led them into a brief affair.

In effect, Robert's lack of trust created the circumstances that nurtured the very betrayal he feared. Essentially, piece by piece, he tore down the bridge that had once united them in intimacy. From Jean's point of view, he had broken the bond of trust with her. Consequently she felt betrayed by *his* mistrust, leading her to turn to someone else.

Had they both been able to confront the underlying mistrust, they might have been able to heal their relationship and restore their bridge before it was too late. I met Robert after Jean was remarried. He was struggling with the risk of trusting others and of letting himself be vulnerable again—the risks needed to gain intimacy and allow love back into his life.

The Roots of Trust

The trust needed for a good relationship—and the betrayal felt when trust fails—is deeply rooted in human nature. It is, in fact, the first developmental task that we as newborns confront soon after birth, when we have to develop a sense of safety based on depending on another person, normally our mother. This early dependency for safety and security creates the first building block for trust since, according to many scholars including Erik Erikson, a leading figure in the field of human development, trust develops out of our earliest experiences of being cared for and protected in a constant and loving way. As a result, if we as infants don't acquire this trust, because, for example, we aren't fed regularly or held lovingly, we may not survive. Without the psychological nourishment that comes from trust, we may stop eating and fail to thrive.

As we become adults, an inability to trust is not usually life threatening, but we still need it to create the bonds for good relationships as well as to gain confidence in ourselves. Trust in others is critical because it forms the underpinnings of our personal security. Take that away, and we are left feeling uncertain not only of others but of our own worth.

Examples abound of what happens when the bonds of trust are broken, such as when we grow up in a home where we feel we can't depend on our parents. Perhaps we are not nurtured properly because of problems with alcohol, drug abuse, or a high level of conflict or domestic violence in the home. We may well grow up feeling especially empty because our emotional needs haven't been satisfied by those closest to us. Without this support we experience a damaged sense of self. As an adult, we may feel especially fragile and be reluctant to trust others out of fear of being hurt again.

Alternatively, we may be more likely to betray others, acting from our own excessive caution or suspicion. Or, in another common scenario, our emotional neediness may cause us to become all-too trusting in a search for love, only to be a devastated victim of repeated betrayal.

In contrast, individuals who grow up in a safe, secure environment have a better foundation for establishing a confident sense of trust in others and themselves, although at all stages of life there are still more challenges. For example, the child starting school may encounter other children who lie or play tricks on the playground. Teenagers may find themselves facing devious game playing at school as the battle over dating heats up and cliques form between those who are in and those who are out. All of us are challenged to negotiate the uncertainties and dangers of the many relationships we develop; we must learn lessons about how and when to trust under varying circumstances. The developmental process is like swimming through unfamiliar waters; we kick carefully as we learn where to avoid the rocks that threaten our safe passage.

The need to trust and be trusted continues throughout the life cycle. At every developmental level, we are more likely to have good relationships and succeed in whatever we do when our relationships are based on trust. In contrast, whenever trust breaks down, as psychologists well know, individual development is inhibited. We can't grow as fully as individuals, and we are less able, even *un*able, to have satisfying love relationships.

Finding love becomes a casualty, because trust is at the foundation of any relationship. Without it, intimacy becomes difficult, if not impossible. We become afraid to open up because we don't feel emotionally safe. We do not allow our vulnerability to become exposed. We avoid opening the keys to our heart, a requirement in love relationships. And so love may never develop, or perhaps it may wither quietly. Ultimately it will be unsatisfactory.

Love-trust is analogous to what happens when you drive a car. Trust is like the accelerator that propels the car. With plenty of trust, you zoom ahead, like a carefree traveler on an open road. You relax, enjoy the scenery, feeling perfectly safe. You know your partner will protect you and help you maneuver along the road, enabling you to enjoy the ride.

But when you and your partner don't trust each other, it is as if you are driving with one foot on the brake as you attempt to accelerate with the other. You want to move ahead, but are afraid because you might veer off the road and crash. Your fear prevents you from enjoying the ride. What's more, you are so frightened of crashing that you don't drive well. The accident you fear looms ahead, just over the next hill.

Developing trust in a love relationship is more intense than in other partnerships. It is like driving a car on a dark road. While each of us can make decisions that will promote the experience of love-trust, it is delicate and gradually forms over time. The acceleration must be paced. It can be strengthened by what we do and say, but it cannot be forced or rushed. It is not prudent to "put the pedal to the metal." We can identify and work toward resolving the obstacles in the path of a growing trust, and provide materials that pave the way; that's all the control we can exert.

Developing a Trust Road Map

Trust issues permeate our lives, but sorting them out is often far from easy. Knowing the road ahead is sure to help. My intent is that this book will offer you a road map pointing the way toward greater trust in love relationships. We will examine every component of trust, including childhood issues that follow us into adulthood, the dynamics of jealousy, dependency fears, relationship breakups, the role of expectations, and sexual betrayal.

Dramatic betrayals—such as infidelity and fraud—make for hot copy. But trust invades our relationships more commonly through much more mundane interactions. These are the interactions that will come under scrutiny in the following pages. We will see, for instance, that trust intersects with reliability: A couple agrees to an eight o'clock bedtime for their son. A few minutes before eight, the father invites the boy to watch the ballgame with him. Isn't the wife justified when she feels let down? Alternatively, should a wife whose otherwise fabulous husband is a notorious procrastinator trust him to get the tickets for the Broadway show? If she does, and he screws up, is this a man in desperate need of a tough-love procrastination seminar or a woman who used poor judgment? After all, she knew he wasn't reliable for time-sensitive things.

And what about our everyday efforts as human beings? Do we have a responsibility to continue to grow, to push those personal boundaries as long as we live? When the husband whose wife is leaving objects, "But I'm the same man you married twenty years ago," and she replies, "Yes, and that's why I'm leaving!" does she have a point? Is a failure to be your best a betrayal of trust? What about trusting a man enough to allow him to see you in an unflattering light? How important is that?

Yet another question: what about those "little white lies"? Do they really matter? Are they harmless or, like psychological termites, is each bite barely perceptible until the floor weakens?

Whether it is the result of a dramatic betrayal or the cumulative effect of many small assaults, trust can break down in love partnerships. This book will discuss what to do to rebuild after the break and heal from the loss.

THE FOUNDATION OF TRUST

Dynamics of Trust and Mistrust

Trust is so basic to a relationship that we may feel deeply wounded if we don't receive it or when we lose it. When this happens, we may not only have doubts about our partner, but the feeling of mistrust can spread like a cancer through every aspect of our lives. We can lose faith in ourselves and our ability to trust. We can lose our trust in others, afraid that we can't count on them. In some cases, we feel terrified that we are losing control over our lives since we don't know where to turn for support.

Imagine a little bird that unwittingly flies into a house and can't get out. It searches for a way back to the garden where it felt safe and secure with what was known and comfortable. It is now in uncertain, even dangerous territory, so when it hears the footsteps and voices of people trying to help it out, it retreats in fear, hiding behind furniture. The only way it can get out is to make itself vulnerable, but it fears that the people who want to help will destroy it. So it wavers, fluttering help-lessly, appearing and retreating, not sure whether to trust in goodness or fear its own end.

The dynamics of trust are much like this. We need to trust, yet many of us are so afraid; like that little bird, we are in unfamiliar territory. Perhaps we have been hurt before and are now timid about exposing ourselves. Yet, like the bird, we need to know when to reveal ourselves in order to get back into the garden. We need to make ourselves vulnerable in the right circumstances if we are going to be able to grow and to love.

Difficulties of Being Able to Trust

Unfortunately, there are many mixed messages about trust in our society. We personally encounter barriers in our own families, with peers as we grow up, and with other adults in our private and work lives. In addition, modern life is simply not conducive to trust.

Examples of inability to trust are everywhere, like erosion that undercuts the very foundation of society. Consider:

- Several U.S. presidents have lied to us. Typically, their slick spokespeople go on national television and smoothly explain away the discrepancy between the truth and the president's statements and actions. We have learned to accept lack of trustworthiness at the highest levels of government. We laugh about the betrayal when comedians make jokes to diffuse our unease.
- We have difficulty trusting our own American media, because of repeated examples of reporters lying and fabricating stories, of TV news programs simulating and exaggerating events, of tabloids and columnists treating speculation as fact.
- We hear repeated stories of authority figures and once-respected moral leaders who have betrayed our trust—priests molesting children, politicians with ties to unsavory crime figures, coaches encouraging performance-enhancing drugs to give players an illegal advantage. Doctors cover up their medical mistakes, lawyers stretch honesty and ethics to win their case, and scientists fake data to promote their career.
- Popular entertainment creates heroes of people who are deceptive, lie, dissemble, or otherwise can't be trusted. Consider a sampler of movie themes from the late '90s: A cagey art thief outcons the investigator out to cheat him. A lovable con man on the lam from jail who charms the FBI agent out to recapture him. A charming, but devious woman leads several men to the

altar, then runs away; the hero who is out to expose her falls for her too. This is just a smattering of lovable rogues glamorized by motion pictures.

- Repeatedly, businesspeople use deceptive strategies, even outright lies, when it is in their interest to get ahead. Recent examples include the behind-the-scenes machinations of Microsoft, the lies of a banker who brought down Barclay's Bank, and the deceptions of inside traders and stock manipulators.

In short, we live in a culture at odds with our personal struggle to seek the trust that provides us with a sense of emotional safety and security.

No wonder so many of us are disillusioned. Yet that is why we desperately need to be able to trust. The more we experience a loss of control in our life and over the societal institutions we depend on, the more we need to find a haven in our intimate relationships.

So where do we find a haven? How do we build the trust we need? Perhaps a good way to begin is with our need for trust, the subtle play of trust in our daily life and the expectations that have to be satisfied for us to feel trust. Then, let's consider what we gain when we have trust. Understanding the importance of trust and what prevents us from achieving it will help prepare us for the steps needed to rebuild broken love.

The Need for Trust

Trust means different things to different people—dependability, loyalty, honesty, fidelity, predictability. But at its heart is feeling physically secure and emotionally safe. When you trust someone, you are able to express your deepest feelings and fears; you reveal who you are, what you want, and what you need, knowing the other person will accept you, regard your feelings, and protect you. In turn, your trusting partner can do the same, knowing you will respond in kind.

In essence, when you trust others and act on that trust, you are giving them a piece of yourself, believing they will be understanding, caring, and honor your faith in them. When they reciprocate, intimacy can grow.

We need trust just as our bodies need the food and water that sustain us. We need trust for emotional sustenance—it is the food for our emotional growth, the water for our spiritual development.

We need to have trust in our love relationships every day. Some people mistakenly think of trust as coming into play only in crises, such as when one partner is accused of sexual infidelity but denies it. However, trust must actually be woven into the entire fabric of the relationship. We need to be able to trust in an all-inclusive way—that a partner will be reliable, honest, keep promises, act in our best interest, maintain confidences, and return our love. While a small, isolated breach of trust may have minor impact, repeated instances can have a cumulative effect.

Everyday Events That Break Down Trust

Most of us are disappointed by a love partner as a result of an everyday event far more often than we are made angry or jealous by a serious and dramatic betrayal. For example, Jeff maintains his friendship with Glen, an old army buddy, in utter secrecy. His wife, Dorothy, has always disliked Glen and has asked Jeff not to see him. Jeff has agreed but is undeterred. "I find a way," he says. "All Dorothy knows is that I'm working late, running an errand or something. We go for a drink, hang out together, that sort of thing. If I told Dorothy, she would raise the roof, so why aggravate her?" What else does Jeff hide to avoid confrontations with Dorothy? And what if Dorothy were to discover Jeff's deception?

Likewise, Margaret explains:

> *During the past few months, I suspected something was wrong with Mike. He kept telling me everything was fine. Last week, out of the blue, he told me there was an investigation at his firm that had been going on for nearly a year and he was named in an indictment. He wanted me to know in case it made the news. I was shocked, but even more shocked that he had not confided in me earlier, that each day he came home and faked it. I feel like the past year was fraudulent. He says he didn't want to worry me. Now I wonder if I can trust him to be honest about anything.*

Her reaction is common. When trust is breached in one area, the disappointed partner often feels unable to trust that person again. That is the power of trust betrayed. It spreads throughout the entire relationship like a deadly toxin.

For instance, Kevin and Janice, who have lived together for the past few years, are on the verge of splitting up because Janice contends that Kevin "never lives up to his word." Here's what Janice has to say about some troubling events:

> *I can't believe anything he tells me anymore. I ask him if he's taken care of the rent for this month and he assures me that he has. The next thing I know, the landlord is calling me and asking me about the rent. Or I ask him to do me a favor. He agrees and then doesn't come through.*

As Janice describes it, when she complained to Kevin about his behavior, their conversation went like this:

KEVIN: *There you go, exaggerating again. Once I was late with the rent. Maybe twice. And I knew you'd bug me if I told you the truth. The same thing with the favors. Sometimes I say yes just so you'll get off my case.*

JANICE: *So now you're telling me that you purposely lie to me and it's my fault because I bug you?*

KEVIN: *I'm just saying that sometimes you drive me crazy, and at those times, especially if I'm feeling tired or something, I'll do anything to get relief.*

JANICE: (sarcastically) *That's great. Now I can never trust what you tell me, because it may be one of those times that you simply want to be left alone or avoid a hassle.*

At this point, Janice explained that she felt so disappointed and insecure by Kevin's lack of candor that she no longer trusted him in any area of their life together and was ready to leave. Kevin pleaded with her to reconsider and she did, on the condition that she and Kevin resolve their differences. Kevin agreed to discuss their relationship and talk honestly about what bothered him as well as to listen to Janice's concerns.

It became clear as Janice and Kevin worked towards a resolution that Kevin had chosen the convenience of "yessing" his partner at the expense of his credibility. By talking openly for the first time, they began to establish a renewed bond of trust.

Another way that trust breaks down is when little deceptions build up over time. One partner may tend to conceal the full price of purchases out of fear that the other partner may consider it extravagant. The purchaser may say, "I bought it at a sale," and trim the price considerably. Other serious forms of deception involve ongoing gambling or drinking. Often people don't speak honestly of the extent of their difficulties with these behaviors.

Yet another trust-eroding practice involves the pretense of admiring the way a partner is dressed: "Oh, yes, I think that jacket looks fine." "No, no. Your stomach doesn't protrude in that outfit." The rationale in such cases is "I don't want to hurt my sweetheart's feelings." But the recipient of false compliments and reassurances can usually see through the deception, and that undermines credibility.

Among the more sensitive areas, sex is particularly important to the development of trust between love partners. How many women have kept the secret that they don't reach orgasm with their partners? How many men have agreed to be sexual with their partners without revealing that they really aren't in the mood? How many women inhibit themselves because they are uncomfortable with their body? In the dating scene, deception is even more common: "You're the first I've ever done that with;" "that was the best I ever had;" "I haven't been with anyone else in years;" "your body is incredible . . . "

Both men and women sacrifice honesty—in this most sensitive of interactions—to bolster their own or their partner's ego or because they are embarrassed by their unresponsiveness. But as long as they do so, they are undermining, rather than building, trust.

In contrast, if a couple were to discuss their feelings honestly and reject the myths that an orgasm, firm behind, or ever-charged libido is the ticket to self-worth, their sex would likely become more fulfilling. It would be transformed from an exercise in mutual game-playing based on deceit to an expression of intimacy.

Why Deception Is So Destructive

Deceptive maneuvers are destructive to a relationship because they sabotage the building of trust. They are barriers that stand in the way of lovers knowing themselves and others.

Many people give a benevolent explanation for their deception, contending that it's for the other person's sake. They think or tell their partner, "I'm doing it to protect you, to make you feel better." But in fact deceivers really protect only themselves. By being deceptive, they avoid confrontations with their partners and continue the gambling, drinking, or whatever else they want to hide. At the same time, they foreclose an open, trusting relationship. In most cases the deceived partner knows or has a hunch that the truth is not being told. As a result, a wall of suspicion separates the partners.

Dangers of Inconsistency and Unreliability

Being inconsistent or unreliable also leads to mistrust, although its ill effects are less obvious than those caused by deception. Inconsistency is present when a partner speaks and acts in contradictory ways. If one partner tells the other, "You are the most important person in my life and my top priority," but in daily behavior is selfish, inconsiderate, and irritable, how can the words be trusted? One may believe that one cares deeply, and such speech is flattering, but one's actions speak more forcefully and belie the words.

In a similar vein, when one partner tells another that "I trust you to handle our finances," yet keeps voicing concern about expenditures, income, and bill payments, this sends a confusing message. Such concerns show doubts that the responsible party will do a good job. So how can the statement that "I trust you" be believed?

Building towards greater honesty and increased trust involves not simply saying what one believes but doing what one says. A person who wants to be counted on must be consistent in both words and behaviors. One must "walk the walk," as they say.

For example, Charlie agreed that he was not giving his relationship sufficiently high priority, that he was neglectful of his partner's desire to have him as a companion. As one part of the solution, he agreed to pick up ballet tickets that evening, an expression of his relationship concern. But he forgot, and since he would break his promises chronically, his partner's disappointment triggered an ugly battle.

For some people, being unreliable becomes a way of life. Frequently, they are moved by temporary feelings of guilt ("She seems so upset about my not being attentive") or require the approval of their partner ("I'd better say yes—he seems angry about this"). Others acquiesce so that their partner will "get off my back." As we've seen with Janice and Kevin, the relief is short-lived, only to be replaced by their partner's rage.

Nothing changes when the "forgetful" partner avoids specifying a time when a promise will be honored: "Yes, I will get the tickets." The recipient of the promise is appeased; but as compliance is delayed, a cycle of nagging and coercion as well as mistrust is likely to pollute the relationship.

The same effect is often produced by vague statements: "I agree that I need to be more attentive" or "OK, I'll be more responsive." In the former case the speaker does not show a willingness to do anything different. The latter statement avoids a specific plan of action; it is likely to be just another New Year's resolution that weakens trust.

On other occasions, suspicion arises not so much by what is said, but by how it is said. For instance, Larry may say, "I'm listening," while glancing at the morning newspaper. Likewise, Allen may say, "I love you," over and over but in a flippant manner with his attention elsewhere. Their partners each have good cause to wonder about the reliability of what they hear.

Whenever words convey a different message from tone of voice or body language, the listener is likely to feel suspicious and confused. An "I love you" is greatly strengthened if one maintains eye contact while speaking. Moving open hands toward one's partner says something very different than clenching one's fists. And sitting with one's knees close together expresses a very different feeling than reaching toward one's partner with open, outstretched legs.

Sometimes a simple assertive statement will do. Larry was obviously more interested in the morning's news than in conversing with his wife, Rita. Larry could have said, "Couldn't we wait till later?" If Rita felt strongly about talking, she could have made this known. If she didn't, she could have respected Larry's desire to delay the conversation.

Larry and Rita were being overly polite in an attempt to create an impression that is unreasonable: We are both *always* desirous of contact with each other. In actuality, both Larry and Rita were collecting resentment—and undermining trust.

Tricky Agreements

The manner in which we make and break agreements also profoundly impacts the state of trust in our relationships. Practically all social relationships involve agreements—whether official or unofficial, tacit or explicit. Agreements govern the ways in which people behave toward each other. In couple relationships, where contact is frequent and covers a wide variety of behaviors, agreements are particularly important. Official agreements, those sanctified by state or religious institutions, usually address the general structure of the marital relationship. For instance, some Christian weddings speak of a duty to "love, honor, and obey." Most couples do not take these obligations seriously until facing a divorce.

Unofficial agreements, however, are usually taken very seriously. Developed by the couples themselves, they are concerned with daily living—how each partner will behave toward the other, and the assignment of responsibilities. Some of these agreements are explicit. For instance, one spouse may offer to fill in by doing the food shopping and, in exchange for this effort, take a few hours later on to play ball. Another may agree to take care of certain chores if other family members cooperate in specified ways. All couples have rules—ongoing agreements—that dictate those actions to be rewarded and those to be ignored or punished.

While some agreements are verbalized, many remain unvoiced. A husband badgers his wife, and when she's had as much as she can take, her hands begin to tremble. He continues pushing, only to propel them into a fierce battle, followed by withdrawal. After this sequence has been repeated a few times, both "know" that trembling hands are a signal to back off. Sex—where, what kind, and how often—is another common area of unspoken agreement. Partners often signal each other without words ("When he shuts the TV off before the late news, I know he's interested"). Sometimes the division of responsibilities also falls into place without a spoken agreement. Whether decided by one's gender, skills, schedule, or some other standard, agreements may be made without discussion.

However, some types of relationship "contracts," as agreements are often called, are drawn up with no intention of carrying them out. One type that wreaks havoc on trust involves making an offer that is withdrawn when the partner accepts. For example, a spouse may suggest taking a day off so that the couple can share intimate time together. The other spouse, having already made plans, nonetheless consents enthusiastically in order to keep such offers coming. Acceptance is then met with an accusation: "How could you be so unconcerned with my career to encourage my absence from work!"

Illicit contracts like that create agony and will most often spawn more of the same. The wife, having been wounded, may devise a game of her own to retaliate. The result is frequently a contract of mutual avoidance—a maneuver that, if continued, often evolves into a formalized contract of divorce.

Yet another crazy-making, trust-eroding ploy casts a long-lasting spell on a couple. In this maneuver, one person suggests that cooperation can be expected. But somehow the subject under discussion manages to change, and the implied promise to cooperate never gets fulfilled. That is, the partner behaves inconsiderately while appearing to be considerate and collaborative. This creates a growing expectation that can slowly drive the expectant partner to distraction:

MATE ONE: *Money is really tight. I would like you to keep the checkbook balanced and up-to-date so that we can monitor our budget.*

MATE TWO: (with a show of concern) *But dear, we've been saving a good deal of money on fuel this winter.*

MATE ONE: (confused) *We have to keep an eye on the checkbook.*

MATE TWO: *Oh, darling, you know how concerned I get about you when you start worrying. Now, what would you like for dinner?*

Mate One goes off to work feeling some tightness in the stomach. A dull ache is beginning between the shoulder blades and moving toward the back of the neck. How could these unsettled feelings relate to such a sweet, caring partner? Mate One is likely to conclude, "There is something wrong with me." In reality, the experience at home was not unlike reaching into a fog. Mate Two responded, but not to the issue that Mate One raised.

While some agreements are obvious trust-busters requiring scrutiny, many are not. In fact, in some instances it is better not to discuss an agreement. Not only would the process be awkward, it could become a source of embarrassment. If Jared offers aloud to do the shopping in exchange for ball-playing time, his wife may feel hurt that he isn't shopping "simply to please me." Or, if Jared and Lorraine have silently agreed that he is the one to initiate sex by turning the TV off at a certain hour, saying so might be embarrassing. Only when there is discord or distrust do agreements need to be reviewed.

Maintaining Trust Through Changing Times

Neither being consistent and reliable nor keeping agreements precludes change. Indeed, a person who remains the same throughout a long-term relationship would become boring to any partner. Change is a given in any relationship. However, to maintain trust, both partners need to be open and aboveboard with each other, so that they know where they stand and can depend on what the other says, *even in changing circumstances.*

Certainly, at times you may not like what your partner says or does. You may feel some distress about certain changes that are occurring. But as long as there is no deception, no betrayal of trust, you can understand this change, adjust to it, and modify yourself or your relationship as needed. In fact, this kind of openness and honesty will make you and your partner better able to respond to change, since you can move ahead with less fear of the unknown.

A good way to deal with the changes you each experience is to not only discuss them, but to recognize that change comes with aging and altered life situations. Frequently, partners mistakenly regard change as a breach of trust and become suspicious. They look on changes in appearance, new attitudes, and new interests as warning signals of moving apart. Consider the following reactions:

- "But you always liked my hair short!" (Does that mean you no longer find me attractive?)
- "How can you say you hate your job? You have always loved it!" (You must be planning something.)

- "What do you mean you don't want to go to the theater? I know you love the ballet!" (What are you up to?)

In all of these examples, trust is undermined when one person fails to accept the other as evolving. It is a setup for feeling disappointed. A partner's no longer acting as one expects does not justify the conclusion: "I can't trust you."

Trust, then, is *not* based on a vow of sameness. We need not pledge: "I hereby agree that I will always believe and behave exactly the way I did when we met." Rather, in a vital relationship, our vows will account for and embrace change. For example, William Lederer and Don Jackson, in *The Mirages of Marriage*, offer this statement as a foundation for trust:

> *We are human beings, and will change and grow with age and circumstances. Neither of us is perfect. We are not afraid of being fallible and therefore we will be honest and open with each other, and reveal ourselves and our changes and failures.... If what happens is joyful (as we have faith it will be most of the time), we will treasure this good fortune. But if events are painful or harmful, we will adjust and accept the changes because it is a fact. Instead of being punitive toward each other, we will be consoling and encouraging.*

Meeting Each Other's Expectations

Whenever we trust someone, we are actually expressing certain expectations about how we want that person to act or feel toward us. Some expectations—being understanding, supportive, faithful, honest, and accepting, for example—are fundamental for trust. However, meeting a lover's expectations can get complicated.

Some people regard only complete fulfillment as being good enough. In pursuit of perfect trust they enter relationships with extreme caution. To these persons, a lover is a lover all the way; total love, support, and trust are ever present, or it is not love at all. Indeed, some of us hold standards set so high that we remain alone, spending our lives separated from others by our cynicism.

In contrast, other people are irresponsible in meeting the reasonable expectations of a loved one. They drift along with others as easy riders, in shallow alliances, blurring the distinction between honesty and dishonesty. They do not see that in the economy of love relationships trust is the currency. You lend it. You save it. The small change is as important as the large bills.

But be clear about your expectations. When they are not conscious, stated, or realistic, it is easy to feel betrayed when you haven't been. Betrayal implies a broken promise; it is not betrayal when no such promise was made. We may have wanted something from a love partner who never agreed to give it. For instance, a woman may marry a man expecting that he will be an integral part of her family of origin. When he fails to *feel* as close to her family as she had visualized, she may feel conned, even though they never discussed the issue.

In another case, a man accuses his lover of disloyalty when she fails to take his side in an argument with a mutual friend. She protests; not only has she been unaware of his concept of loyalty, she can cite an instance in which he did the same thing to her.

Then there are truly unreasonable expectations: a partner who really loves you should be able to read your mind; real lovers never disagree; being in love always feels a certain way; you shouldn't have to work at trust; your partner should be emotionally available to you at all times; and your partner should forgive your flaws (but not the other way around).

You may expect your partner to measure up to your "super" parent. Alternatively, you may expect your spouse to be like your difficult parent was and let you down. You may expect your marriage to resemble your parents' blissful connection, or a *Cosmopolitan* view of bliss. In contrast, you may expect very little, and therefore give very little. In relationships based on romanticized beliefs and images, pain results not because there has been a breach of actual trust, but because of all-out trust in ideas that were wrong to begin with.

When feelings of betrayal slip into your relationship, check out your expectations. Scrutinize everything you expect, the tangibles (taking out the garbage, sharing the carpooling of the kids on the weekends) and the intangibles (emotional support, openness, etc.).

Instead of stewing over disappointments, evaluate them. If your relationship doesn't live up to your ideas about love, the problem may not be with your relationship but with your ideas.

In addition, unless there has been a major and devastating breach of trust, it is useful to view a violation of an expected trust this way: each time trust is strengthened it is as if a deposit is made in a relationship account. Each deposit increases hope; and confidence in the future builds. Deposits also compound trust, like interest in a money account. In a trust account an accumulation of trustworthy acts creates the attitude, "You think well of me and try to please me; I will do the same."

What's more, an account that has many trust deposits can withstand occasional withdrawals of trust, such as when you have minor slipups, like the white lie to cover up for a forgotten birthday. Deposits buffer the sting of disappointment.

Certainly, some small withdrawals are inevitable. But it is only when your account is depleted or overdrawn that you start to lose hope. And if hope dwindles enough, the relationship can become bankrupt.

What We Gain from Trust

When our expectations of trust are reasonably fulfilled, our gains are bountiful in several areas:

- our feeling of self-respect and well-being;
- our sense of personal safety, because we feel we have a trusted partner by our side looking out for our welfare;
- our sense of intimacy, because we can reveal ourselves knowing our vulnerabilities and weaknesses will be accepted; and
- our ability to love more fully, more richly, more deeply.

In short, the process of becoming trustworthy and working out the trust issues with your partner enhances your growth. You will become more satisfied with yourself. You will be more likely to evolve into a multidimensional, more mature person. And you will also end up walking the tightrope of love with more balance and perspective.

RECOGNIZING 2 TRUST . . .
AND MISTRUST

Trust is tricky. What shakes one person's faith—a tendency to exaggerate, for instance—may not even register as an issue for someone else. Nor are trust troubles always apparent. Some trust fissures burst open and swallow us whole before we know what happened.

It's comforting to know that our love partner is trustworthy. But what if we aren't so confident? What if we feel uneasy? Are there red flags we should recognize? But maybe it's us. Perhaps we are putting up barriers, making it difficult for our partner to trust and confide in us.

For Karen, thirty-five years old, the problem of trust came up when her husband, Larry, the owner of a small company, had to take occasional business trips lasting 3–4 days. She accepted the necessity of the trips to meet with prospective clients, yet she worried that he might be attracted to another woman when he was away. Even though he called her each morning and evening to report on the progress of his trip, she remained nervous. When she mentioned her concerns, Larry was reassuring.

By the second year, Karen was confident and appreciated how Larry took her concerns so seriously. He loved her as much as ever, she told herself. Then, during one of his out-of-town calls, Larry mentioned that he had brought his new marketing assistant along. He wanted to train her to make pitches to clients herself.

At once, Karen's alarm signal blared. She had met Larry's new assistant, Judy, and thought of the younger, attractive, ambitious woman as too available. She imagined Larry and the young woman sharing drinks and dinner with a prospective client, and then perhaps sharing even more later. She felt very nervous when Larry called her after dinner to say that he had gone back to his room with Judy to work on marketing plans for a client the next morning.

Karen became frantic with worry. Yet she concealed her feelings, anticipating that he would become angry if she confronted him. Instead, she decided to wait until he returned home to see if he acted any differently.

Larry returned home late, after Karen had fallen asleep. Not wanting to wake her, he quietly slipped into bed and fell asleep too.

When he woke he told her that Judy worked out so well that he would be traveling much less. "And," he added, "her fiancé is a writer free to travel with her, so that won't be a problem." "Her fiancé?" Karen asked, pleasantly surprised. "Oh, yeah," Larry said casually, "he's a great guy. He came along and brought his laptop. They spent every free minute together."

If Karen had expressed her misguided suspicions in an emotional outburst, there probably would have been angry accusations, righteous denials, and tears. The relationship may have been damaged, with one partner misreading the signs of trouble and the other becoming disturbed by false accusations.

What if the trust issue were money? It is not uncommon for one partner to mistrust the other because of secrecy about finances. Perhaps one partner holds back because of doubts about the solidity of the relationship.

This was the problem for Gail and Howie when they got engaged after dating for several months. One evening, as they were talking about marriage plans, Gail asked Howie about his finances. Instead of telling her straightforwardly what he earned and about his assets, Howie became guarded and defensive. He felt Gail was prying inappropriately and worried that her questions suggested that she was more interested in his money than in him.

"Why are you so secretive?" Gail asked, wondering about his commitment to her. "We're planning to spend the rest of our lives together, aren't we?"

Howie felt even more pressured by her probing and became even more defensive. "I think it's premature for that kind of questioning. We're not married yet," he snapped.

Gail responded by retreating, not wanting to anger Howie further. The exchange left her feeling unjustly shut off, while Howie was left suspicious of her unease.

Withholding important information from one's partner can strike at the heart of a relationship; these are instances when one person keeps secret certain very personal information or a double life, even criminality. Disclosure generally shocks the uninformed partner.

That's what happened to Katherine, after she had been married to Jack, a prosperous businessman, for eight years. One day, returning from work, he suddenly announced, "I'm declaring bankruptcy. My business is hemorrhaging money and there's no other way to stop it." He explained that his firm had been under great financial pressure for a year and he wanted to tell her before she read about it.

Jack's revelation hit her like a bolt of lightning; she felt betrayed that he hadn't told her sooner. She had been aware that he had been preoccupied and inattentive for the last few months, and she had believed him when he explained that he just had some difficult problems at work. His seemingly reasoned explanation led her to think he meant something routine, not a major financial disaster. What else might he have lied about? What else was there he might not have told her?

As these stories illustrate, it's vital to recognize the early signs of trust trouble, the trust distress signals. This allows the opportunity either to honor trust, correct false perceptions, or openly confront real problems before mistrust becomes worse.

Measuring the Level of Trust

So how much trust do you have in your own relationship? What level of trust do you share with your partner? If you find it difficult to answer the question and measure trust, join the club. Trust issues aren't always visible in a relationship. That's why I developed the Trust Scale, an inventory you can use to assess how much you trust your partner. Or you can take it together with your partner to learn how much you trust each other.

Using the Trust Scale

The Trust Scale is designed to be a basis for discussion with your partner about trust issues. It is not a precise scientific instrument. (A brief scale can't capture all of the nuances involved.)

To use the scale, read each statement and indicate how well it applies to your feelings about your partner or your relationship. Then add up the numbers to get your total trust score, and look at your overall pattern of responses. This will give you a picture of the overall level of trust in your relationship, as well as the areas in which it is strongest and weakest. (Discussion on interpreting your scores follows at the end of the scale.)

THE TRUST SCALE

A Starting Point for Discussion

Rate the level of trust you feel in your relationship for each of the following areas by circling the number that most closely reflects your view. Don't take time to think about each response; just put down the first reaction that comes to mind. You will have a chance to analyze your responses after you complete the scale, and you can then discuss your responses with your partner.

	RARELY TRUE	OCCASIONALLY TRUE	FREQUENTLY TRUE	ALMOST ALWAYS TRUE
I. I feel my partner's behavior is straightforward. I can take it at face value.	1	2	3	4

	RARELY TRUE	OCCASIONALLY TRUE	FREQUENTLY TRUE	ALMOST ALWAYS TRUE
2. I consider my partner reliable. I don't expect my partner to disappoint me.	1	2	3	4
3. I trust my partner to keep our agreements. My partner only makes promises that she or he can keep.	1	2	3	4
4. My partner is truthful. My partner does not lie or otherwise try to deceive me.	1	2	3	4
5. I feel my partner is willing to listen receptively and take me seriously when I want to discuss personal and relationship issues.	1	2	3	4
6. My partner knows and understands my views on things that are important to me.	1	2	3	4
7. I feel my partner *really* listens to what I have to say and is able to empathize with me and look at things from my point of view.	1	2	3	4
8. I feel I can confide in my partner on a regular basis, about small everyday things, as well as major issues.	1	2	3	4

	RARELY TRUE	OCCASIONALLY TRUE	FREQUENTLY TRUE	ALMOST ALWAYS TRUE
9. I feel comfortable bringing up topics about which we disagree—I'm not afraid these disagreements will cause serious tensions that could hurt our relationship.	1	2	3	4
10. If my partner and I fight, we can make up quickly and sincerely, because my partner doesn't remain angry and carry a grudge, and neither do I.	1	2	3	4
11. I don't think my partner would withhold any important information from me.	1	2	3	4
12. I can trust my partner to tell me what is really going on. My partner is sincere and genuine in expressing feelings.	1	2	3	4
13. I feel comfortable when my partner participates in outside activities when I am not present. I don't believe my partner would be unfaithful.	1	2	3	4
14. I feel comfortable that, when traveling alone, my partner will continue to be faithful.	1	2	3	4

	RARELY TRUE	OCCASIONALLY TRUE	FREQUENTLY TRUE	ALMOST ALWAYS TRUE
15. I believe my partner is sincerely concerned with my well-being and considers my interests when making decisions that affect us both.	1	2	3	4
16. My partner accepts responsibility for his or her part in our relationship issues.	1	2	3	4
17. I feel my partner regards me as an equal and treats me with respect.	1	2	3	4
18. I feel very comfortable with my partner sexually; we have a strong emotional connection and commun- icate comfortably about sexual matters.	1	2	3	4
19. I trust my partner to handle money matters competently, openly, and fairly.	1	2	3	4
20. I am comfortable making a continued emotional investment in my relationship, because I feel confident we have a strong mutual commitment.	1	2	3	4

Your Overall Score: How Much Trust Do You Feel in Your Relationship?

Add up your score for each question. Possible overall scores range from 20 to 80. Consider your score high if it's over 60; low if it's below 30. In general, the higher your score, the more you trust your partner.

If you are in the group of high scorers, you feel you are in a successful relationship where you are free to be yourself.

Should you have a low score, regard that as an indication that your relationship needs to be improved. It doesn't mean the relationship is hopeless, just in need of repair.

What Your Answers Mean

1. Consistency

A high response suggests your partner's actions and words are consistent. You can trust what is evident; you don't have to worry about hidden agendas. You don't have to feel as if you need a private detective, or be one, to find out what is really going on.

Inconsistency breeds suspicion. This is what nearly derailed Abbey's marriage. She felt she couldn't trust Max's explanations of what he was doing, so she went through his pockets, listened in on his phone conversations, and read his mail. Naturally, Max was disturbed— "Abbey's a snoop," he complained. As a result, he sought to hide even more things from her. He even hid little day-to-day things, like unexpected luncheon meetings with colleagues at work. Secretiveness only fueled Abbey's suspicions. In turn, her suspicions made Max feel like he wanted to throw in the towel.

2. Reliability and Dependability

Your response indicates the extent to which you can depend on your partner when it counts. Dependence and reliance develop over time. For example, your partner calls when promised. Or takes care of the bills each month as agreed. More important, you have learned you can depend on your partner in situations where you would feel hurt or rejected if let down.

Without reliability, relationships can deteriorate. That's what happened to Judith, who described why she decided to leave her husband, John. "I married him because we have a wonderful chemistry. The sex is great. He is intelligent, dynamic, fun to be with. But I can't trust him to keep his word or uphold his end of the family responsibilities. He let me down too often."

3. Keeping Agreements

Trust is definitely strengthened when your partner's promises are fulfilled. Conversely, a failure to keep promises erodes trust. Credibility is shattered. The process of trusting becomes a lottery, where you start asking, will it pay off this time or not?

The doubts that build up over small broken promises can lead to doubts about larger agreements. One woman wondered about her husband, "What other promise will he fail to keep? How do I know that our agreement to be faithful to each other won't become another one of his broken promises?"

4. Honesty

A major trust builder is knowing you can count on your partner's statements to be true and not misleading. This means you expect your partner to be truthful, but also to be complete. Leaving out important information is a lie of omission. Slick, evasive statements leave you standing on ever shifting sand.

For example, Clare felt her salesman husband used his work tactics at home to persuade her to take his point of view: "If he wants to go to the mountains on a vacation and I don't want to, he'll build up the place he wants to visit, make it seem so much better than it is, so it sounds great. In one instance, he said something was very close to town, so I wouldn't feel isolated. But it turned out to be miles away."

If you start feeling you can't trust what your partner is saying, or not saying, then you need to discuss this.

5. Being Emotionally Open and Receptive

Having an emotionally supportive relationship is vital to building trust; given emotional support and understanding, we expose more of ourselves. Sharing, when combined with our partner's willingness to be self-disclosing, is the key to intimacy. Conversely, when emotional receptivity isn't present, we may hold back. We may even find conversation diminishing to brief exchanges. And if you experience long periods of silence, that's a warning sign—something is seriously wrong.

That was Alice's complaint. She stated, "My husband and I haven't had a real conversation in years. When I did confide in him, he wasn't interested. He thinks we have a perfect marriage now, because we never argue. But how can we argue when we don't talk about anything more than the kid's soccer games and grades?"

6. Feeling Understood

Most of us want a partner who not only listens, but also demonstrates understanding. Over time, you expect your sweetheart to know your views on important issues as well. Otherwise, the fire of love and passion may become dampened by resentment. Your anger is likely to be the result of feeling that you are not important enough to your partner.

That's how Carolyn felt when she told Simon that she wanted to leave her job because she hated it, and he responded by criticizing her judgment rather than showing support. As she explained:

> When I told Simon I wanted to devote all my time to pursuing the acting career I'd always wanted, his first reaction was total silence. Then he told me I was unstable. He criticized my poor judgment. I didn't feel he needed to agree with my decision. But I expected him to understand how frustrated I was with my job and my life.

7. Having Empathy

When feelings are identified and expressed in an empathic manner, a couple will sometimes find that the real difficulty has little to do with what they are arguing about. A fight about flirting at social gatherings, for instance, might only be a symptom of assumptions: "If you loved me, you wouldn't do this" or "If you respected me, you'd trust me." The fears behind the assumption are quite similar: "I'm afraid you don't love me/trust me." At this level, seeming differences turn into shared experiences; each partner might feel threatened by the flirting or the command to stop. The surface disagreement may express the differences in the way each partner avoids or copes with similar feelings. Only via empathy will a couple achieve a level of discussion in which these discoveries will occur.

8. Sharing Confidences

When you trust, you can share personal views with your partner, both small everyday matters and larger revelations. It is comforting to know that your partner is willing not only to listen, but also to safeguard your disclosures. It's especially important to feel you can trust your partner to maintain confidentiality.

Unfortunately, Sandy didn't feel that way. After five years of marriage, she decided not to tell her husband the secrets her friends tell her. "He forgets they're confidential," she said. "And though he swears he won't say anything, he forgets and I'm floored." Where once there had been an easy flow of conversation, now there's a strain.

9. Feeling Safe During Disagreements

In any relationship, conflict can flourish like germs in a biology class petri dish. That's because daily closeness increases the potential for disagreement and conflict over even small matters. However, those who try too hard to deny these disagreements, or are afraid to bring them up, end up with a shell of a relationship.

On the other hand, for some couples, bringing up sensitive issues produces an explosion. It can lead to wounded feelings and even wounded people. As a result, couples may move further apart, like islands with a widening channel between them.

This kind of fear is what led Maria to break up with Jimmy. She couldn't discuss anything without risking a war of words. "Jimmy never hit me," she said, "but he got really angry when we argued. He got this crazy look in his eyes and punched holes in the wall. I kept worrying that he would start punching me as well. Eventually, I couldn't take it anymore and broke up with him. Only after I left, several weeks later, did I realize just how tense I had become around him."

10. Confidence in Resolving Disagreements

The German philosopher Arthur Schopenhauer told the story of two porcupines huddled together on a cold winter's night. As the temperature dropped, the animals moved closer together. But then there was a problem: Each kept getting pricked by the other's quills. Finally, with much shifting and shuffling and changing positions, they managed to work out an equilibrium. Each got maximum warmth with a minimum of painful pricking from the other. Many couples have much in common with these huddling porcupines. They want to achieve warmth and closeness but also want to avoid getting jabbed.

For some, it doesn't work out. Ellen felt a growing distance with her husband John that she was afraid to bridge. As she explained, "John has taught me to avoid difficult issues between us. If I bring up something he doesn't want to discuss, he storms off, leaving me feeling guilty and abandoned. He has acted like this so often, I have just shut down. I'm afraid to bring up anything that might provoke a fight. It makes me feel very lonely and unsure of our relationship."

11. Openness in Sharing Information

Complaining about "communication problems" is fashionable. Yet many couples—influenced by the folklore of romantic love—believe that an innate sensitivity should link them and their partner. Being in a relationship, some contend, affords them the privilege of being less diligent in their efforts to communicate than they might be in casual contacts. In effect, they say, "You ought to know how I feel or what I mean if you really love me."

Unfortunately, most people do not read minds. One of the most thought-provoking results of the considerable research in this area is how little husbands and wives really do know or understand one another. "I know him like the back of my hand," brags one partner. But under experimental conditions (described by psychologist John Gottman and his colleagues) their performance more closely resembles the bloopers of couples on the "Newlywed Game."

It's a good thing Jan and Henry weren't contestants. "I'm usually the last one to know when anything happens," Jan complained. "Henry hides himself behind his paper or the TV at night and rarely talks. One day he lost his job. I didn't know for a week. I only found out when a job counselor called saying he had a promising lead."

12. Being Sincere and Genuine

Imagine that you are at a party, listening to an attractive person—and you're beginning to fidget. It's not that you're bored. He is charming and so smooth that you finger your valuables to make sure they're still there.

That is the kind of impression some people make. They seem to know just what to say at the right time, yet they don't feel quite sincere, like the glib politician or persuasive salesperson.

Sometimes they don't seem genuine because their actions belie their words. Or we sense something amiss from their nonverbal cues, like tone of voice, posture, gestures, eye contact, or gaze. Something feels off.

That's what happened to Jamie, who began reassessing her relationship with her husband as her feeling of trust in him declined. She stated, "Everyone thinks my husband is wonderful. He makes them feel like the most important person in the room for the moment. He has enormous charisma. But I've learned that he doesn't mean most of what he says. I'm not sure I want to continue to live like that."

13. Trusting Your Partner When You're Apart

Relationship tension lessens if you can give your partner the space to freely take part in activities without you, expecting loyalty. Everyone needs interests outside a relationship. Interests help us to feel more fulfilled and usually add to the partnership.

If you feel anxious about your partner's outside activities, maybe your partner has really done something to merit mistrust. But consider whether you are perhaps being overly sensitive because of your own doubts. Doubts can come from many sources. For instance, when your partner does something without you, do you feel abandoned or neglected? Do you interpret that need for time alone as a rejection? Do you fear your partner might be saying: "I don't like being with you anymore. I find you boring and want to be independent of you"? Other sources of fear include the belief that you aren't important enough, or that your partner will find someone new.

14. Trusting Your Partner During Extended Absences

Perhaps your partner has to travel extensively for work. Or perhaps one of you wants to go on a vacation and the other can't, or doesn't want to, go. When time apart becomes extended, fear about abandonment, being neglected, and rejection may come up. The feeling may be more intense than in brief separation because of the longer absence.

As Sylvia remarked, "Whenever James goes on a sales trip, I can't help but imagine him with all those younger, attractive women. And it makes me feel older and uninteresting. I feel like I have to compete and I'm at an unfair advantage."

15. Believing Your Partner Has Your Well-Being at Heart

An active concern for the growth and satisfaction of a love partner means that the concerned individual thinks about and does things to promote the other's well-being. Behaviors viewed as supportive may, of course, vary from person to person. Aleesa, a forty-four-year-old artist, married twenty years, expressed her views:

> For me, caring requires the truth. If the quality of my work is disappointing, for example, I don't want someone to rationalize for me or entertain me into a frozen smile; someone who cares doesn't deny my feelings. I want, instead, someone who will listen carefully and try to understand. My husband doesn't do that. He is so caught up in his business that he simply dismisses my concerns out of hand: "Oh, don't worry, things will work out." I feel as if I hardly exist in his life. I've adjusted to that, but it saddens me and limits the relationship.

16. Taking Personal Responsibility

Perhaps the greatest obstacle to improving a relationship is the tendency to blame one's partner for the discord. When things aren't satisfactory, both partners know who's at fault. Just ask them—it's the other person! In order to right things, all that remains (as far as each spouse is concerned) is enlightenment, that is, for the other person to see the light, confess being at fault, and atone. It never works. In fact, when we assign responsibility for our malaise to another person, we impede our own change energy and become a victim.

A certain husband is a poor manager of money. His debts pile up. His major avenue of recovery would be to file for a substantial income tax refund dating back several years. He procrastinates despite his wife's pleading. Finally, after more financially difficult months, he files—and it is too late; the IRS informs him that the cutoff date has passed. He then blames his wife for not pestering him enough. Over time, he continues to deny personal responsibility and escalates the blame: "If it was that important to you," he says, "why didn't you lock me out of the house until I filed the return?" Is this the kind of attitude that engenders trust?

17. Feeling Respected

Even when you strongly differ with your partner, if you respect each other's viewpoints, values, and feelings, you can maintain a strong, intimate bond. Although they may make things more difficult, your differences don't have to undermine your intimacy. You can agree to disagree.

By contrast, if your partner regularly rejects your feelings, thoughts, and actions, you will almost surely feel diminished and alienated. You may find yourself preoccupied with protecting and defending yourself; in time you'll probably begin to withhold when you think your partner will disagree. You will then communicate less and may grow apart.

That's what happened to Joanne, who said, "When I don't think the same way as Joe about politics or social issues, he puts me down. He says I don't understand or I haven't done enough homework on the issue. He has no respect for my views unless they conform to his own."

18. Desiring Sex and Feeling Comfortable with It

While there's no ready formula for connecting sexually, being able to "relax and enjoy each other," as one man put it, certainly helps. In order to do this, a couple has to go beyond the physical experience; without the intimate exchange of thoughts, feelings, and desires, even the most fiery of sexual relationships will soon dry up. Feelings of closeness and distance cannot be divorced from sexual satisfaction; a couple's relationship out of bed cannot be separated from what happens to them in bed.

In effect, sexual satisfaction often corresponds to the degree of non-sexual satisfaction within the relationship.

19. Handling Money Fairly and Openly

Money, like sex, is another area of great sensitivity. Surrounded by loads of expectations, it is part of an exchange based on giving or taking away power. Sometimes the person who controls the money views it as a source of power and prestige, while the other partner feels put down, diminished, and controlled. By contrast, when money matters are shared and discussed openly, the relationship is more egalitarian.

Usually conflicts about money indicate trust problems and can take many forms. Your partner might withhold money, lie about income and expenses, spend too much and undermine the family budget, or in contrast, be too frugal.

Ron was surprised with a money deception and it didn't leave him happy. As he described it:

> My wife keeps the checkbook. I didn't know we had huge outstanding credit card balances until my card was declined when I tried to charge an emergency auto repair. She blamed the credit card company, saying it must be a mistake. But after I insisted she show me the bills and bank statements, I saw the extent of the disaster. We were in debt way over our heads, and I felt I had been betrayed and violated by her overspending.

20. Feelings of Loyalty and Confidence in the Future

Finally, if we feel encouraged, we feel loyal and committed to our partner. We are willing to put in the energy and effort because we are making a long-term investment.

Of course, none of us can predict the future nor be certain that love will endure. But we do need a reasonable sense of basic stability. The promise of continued togetherness enhances a feeling of safety.

In contrast, if there are serious doubts about the endurance of the relationship, it can lead to withholding and retreating, as happened to Ellen. She had been involved in a live-in relationship with Josh, but found herself pulling away when he resisted making a commitment of marriage. When Josh asked her what he had to do to make her feel comfortable enough to be sexually responsive again, Ellen shot back her reply. "I'm sorry, but my days of sex in an uncommitted relationship are in the past," she said, adding:

> *Every time we have a disagreement, you voice concerns about our relationship. I feel it could be over between us at any moment. So I want a commitment from you. I want you to introduce me to your friends. I want to meet your family. I want to feel secure we have a future together or I can't respond.*

Although Josh didn't understand what Ellen's requests had to do with sex, they had everything to do with it. She needed to be sure she could trust a future with him in order to let go.

Using the Trust Scale with Your Partner

Discuss each item of the Trust Scale with your partner. You don't have to make him or her fill out the quiz. Instead, view the questions as a set of focused talking points.

Use the questions in any order and don't feel you have to discuss all of them. Some people don't like responding to a question-and-answer format; they prefer a free-form discussion. Use whatever structure feels best for you.

Lastly, take into account the differences in the way you and your partner respond to questions based on your culture, personality, and gender.

Background and Experience

Trust issues can be shaped by background and by experience. For example, your partner, if having grown up in an alcoholic household, may have learned to expect promises to be made and not kept, because the alcoholic parent was irresponsible and unreliable. In relationship with you, your partner may be especially sensitive and quick to anger if you make a minor misstep, such as coming home later than you said or forgetting to complete a task. Your action triggers a memory of early disappointments, provoking your partner's fear about the solidity of your relationship.

The same kind of problem can occur after a bad experience, such as a woman whose former partner repeatedly cheated on her. She may be especially suspicious of her current boyfriend, asking many prying questions that could turn his love into a desire to pull away and get space.

If the ghosts of past relationships are spooking your present one, you need to recognize them and take them into account.

Male-Female Differences

Men and women often differ on a number of trust issues. These differences come into play when men and women enter into love relationships with each other. For example, on the issue of what's private and what can be shared, women tend to be more liberal, thinking it's fine to tell a close friend about the intimate details of one's love life or a conflict. By contrast, a man may consider those disclosures a privacy violation.

Men also tend to be more reticent to communicate intimately. They are more comfortable acting rather than talking about something, leading a woman to think he is withholding important information when he feels he is not. Conversely, a man may judge a woman's attitudes toward something based on what she does, rather than what she says, since he is action-oriented. So he may not take what she says seriously.

Then, too, men and women have different expectations about closeness and intimacy. Women may be seeking more intimate sharing, while a man may feel she is being too intrusive and needy. He may want more of a sense of separation and space. Boundary questions like these need to be negotiated, based on each partner's expectations and needs.

Additionally, men and women may deal with resolving conflict differently. Often men are less in touch with their emotions or don't want to express strong feelings because they believe emotional expression isn't manly or they fear they will lose control, even become violent, if they release their emotions. But most women can handle intense feelings if they are expressed openly. It is withdrawal and underlying rage that disturbs them the most.

The Importance of Bringing Trust Issues into the Open

Dealing with trust issues is always difficult and emotional. It is not only distressing to mistrust your partner, but it is disturbing when your partner mistrusts you. In addition, some people are hypersensitive to any hint of betrayal, making the issue even searing.

However, while discussing trust problems can be upsetting, it is better than the alternative. Letting mistrust fester and further weaken the relationship will eventually destroy it. So if you can join your partner in honestly exchanging your feelings and beliefs without placing blame, you can go a long way toward understanding your conflicts and the barriers between you. You can develop a plan of action to contain the problems and start working on resolving them.

Generally, your partner will also want an improved relationship and want to cooperate. However, if your partner is resistant because of discomfort dealing with difficult issues or is too busy or unaware to realize there is a problem, begin working for improvement alone. It is better to proceed yourself than to be mired in an impasse.

The way to begin is simple. Seek to be the role model of the kind of person you want your partner to become. Provide an example for him to follow. As a role model, *you* make the first move to reach out and become closer. *You* show more understanding and compassion and trustworthiness.

There's no guarantee that modeling the behavior you want will produce positive results. But you have a far greater chance of getting your partner to reciprocate than if you did nothing. Think of it this way: You are creating an environment in which your partner is most likely to fulfill your needs; if nothing comes of it, at least you'll know you did your part.

THE DEVELOPMENT OF TRUST
IN THE FAMILY

Climbing the Mountain of Trust

As we grow up, we learn trust or mistrust based on how our parents treat us as well as by our early experiences with other family members and peers. The more experiences we have with people we can count on, the more we learn to trust and feel confident in others and ourselves. Conversely, as we encounter disappointments with the people closest to us, trust may become more complicated in our adult lives.

The experience of learning to trust or mistrust is a little like what happens when you are a first-time rock climber on an expedition led by an experienced guide. As a novice, you may be uncertain and scared, unsure of what lies over the ledge of a tall rock formation, or worried that you might fall. Your guide is reassuring; and you feel comforted by your guide's experience and past success with you. Your trust allays your fears. You depend on your guide for your safe ascent and descent, indeed your very survival.

If your trip goes smoothly, it affirms your successful ability to trust. Consequently, you are that much more ready to trust in the future.

In contrast, if in the past your guide was unreliable or the group got lost, you will be less likely to trust this time. Or suppose your guide has made fun of you or pressured you to go too fast, too soon—that would also make you wary. Mistrust might lead you to hold back and not perform well. Or it might lead you to cancel the trip. Or then again, your mistrust might come into play during the journey, leaving you fearful of going any farther, unable to cross a ledge that leads to the only way down.

In any case, with your judgment clouded by mistrust, you will have difficulty climbing at all. A wrong move that could lead to disaster would be more likely. Negative experiences will also color other opportunities to climb, even with a more trustworthy guide. Burned in the past, you are less apt to trust the trail up ahead.

Growing up is like being that rock climber. When we are very young, we depend on our parents and elders for everything, much as the novice climber depends on the guide. We know little and are weak and vulnerable. We must depend on those who are stronger and more knowledgeable as we face an unfamiliar world. Without adult protectors, we can easily get hurt, even killed.

If the adults we depend on prove untrustworthy because they are not reliable, don't care, place us in harm's way, or don't protect us, we get hurt. And we feel increasingly insecure. We start learning to mistrust.

As mistrust builds up, much like the hapless rock climber, we look for ways to protect ourselves. We devise defense mechanisms to shield us against future violations of trust. Such patterns of behavior help us feel emotionally safe, much as the climber might cower in a cave until the rescue party comes.

Once these defense mechanisms begin to function, our life experiences may become less fulfilling. Consequently, we put on even more armor. These mechanisms become set in place and usually continue into adulthood, even when no longer needed. They are like the hardened shell surrounding the turtle. They protect, but the shell is so heavy that it slows us down. Meanwhile, those who trust rapidly pass us by.

How Our First Years Shape Our Relationships

Marsha and Richard had trouble for years because Marsha had a warm, outgoing, trusting nature, while Richard's style was to hold back, afraid to show his true feelings. As a child, Richard learned to suppress his feelings in his family's emotionally hostile environment. He had to work on overcoming the ghosts of mistrust to create a more intimate, trusting relationship with Marsha.

Marsha, thirty-one and a recent college graduate, worked part-time as a laboratory technologist. She had been married for six years to Richard, a part-time pharmacist. They both shared the rearing of their two young children; part-time work gave each of them that opportunity. Yet at times they felt distant from each other, because Richard would retreat into a shell of silence when something bothered him. Typically, Marsha would get angry because Richard wasn't telling her what was wrong. Their conflict was clearly related to their very different upbringings. Marsha described growing up in her family:

We fought often in my family. You could hear us four blocks away. But then I remember many of the fights between my parents or between me and my sister being followed by making up. We said things to each other in anger, but then we apologized for them. Apologies came easily in my family. Also, when I was a child and my parents were mad at me, they told me: "Being angry doesn't mean we don't love you." They told me the same thing was true when they were mad at each other. They both reassured me: "We may disagree about some things and feel very angry, but that doesn't mean we hate each other. We still love each other very much."

Knowing that love was there despite the tears and anger was very important to me. They taught me that a person may not like *something about you, but they will* still *like you. They taught me that love endures despite the conflicts you experience with one another. This lesson has made a critical difference in my relationships. That's why getting angry and speaking my mind isn't as traumatic to me as it is to many of my women friends. I know, on a deep emotional level, that I don't have to be pleasing to others all the time. I can risk disapproval. Rejection doesn't make me feel worthless. I'm not afraid of being wrong or possibly incurring somebody's wrath. I've seen that wrath occur in my own family when I was growing up, and it's not so terrible.*

In contrast to the support Marsha experienced in her family, Richard described a more hostile, nonsupportive environment that led him to feel mistrust not only of his original family, but of his new family with Marsha. That's what led him to retreat at times. Richard explained:

I like Marsha's folks and can see how the safe environment they created was helpful for her. I think she was fortunate to grow up in a home where her parents didn't believe in facades or threaten to reject her for expressing herself. And when I met them, I found her parents to be very real. They openly said what they thought, and didn't try to censor themselves or display only their best side.

My parents are very different. I grew up in a household where they were always bickering, picking on each other for little things, and there was an atmosphere of hostility, even when they weren't openly fighting. There were all these negative feelings that weren't expressed, because the display of emotion was taboo.

As a result of this atmosphere, I picked up a lot of bad habits. For example, unlike Marsha who will say exactly what she thinks, my tendency is to withdraw when something bothers me. I would usually stew about something rather than confront her. Or if I did say something, I said it to make her feel guilty. I realize now that I was trying to get through to her by using emotional blackmail, which is what my family did when I was growing up. None of us trusted one another enough to suspend our defenses and reveal our real feelings. That's because in my family you never knew when someone was going to stab you in the back. And what made the fear even worse was the attack usually came when you least expected it, when your defenses were down. I remember one time—at what seemed like a happy family gathering—the day ended in a barrage of insults.

This environment led me to become very guarded. It was as if a warning notice was posted in my house that read: "Anything you say may be used against you." So I reacted by hiding my real feelings and thoughts. But by doing so, I pulled back at the times when Marsha needed me to be open, and this disparity between Marsha's style and mine made for quite a series of conflicts. Marsha would feel that something was wrong, that I was bothered by something, but I wouldn't tell her, and that would make her think the problem was even worse. She would become upset and we would fight.

It's only in the last year that I have begun to trust, mainly by seeing how Marsha does it and finding that she will accept it when I tell her what's wrong. So I've learned that it's safe to speak up and say what I want and what's bothering me. I realize it's better not to hold back and beat around the issues. And that's helped us both not only deal with the problems, but become closer in our relationship.

Richard's story illustrates what happens when a child believes that love will be withheld if certain feelings or thoughts are expressed. It doesn't matter if parents withhold that love from the child or from each other. In either case the message is that open expression can lead to the loss of love. As a result, before long, the child finds ways to avoid being directly expressive.

For example, if we hear from our parents that "only babies cry," we learn to suppress our feelings of distress by stoically controlling our emotions. Or we show anger to mask our underlying fears and sadness. When we are young, we may also think to ourselves, "I'll get into trouble if I cry" or "If they find out, they'll make fun of me."

As adults we may continue with that line of thinking, though our rationalizations become more sophisticated. We may say to ourselves something like this:

- "I'm being overly sensitive. I shouldn't feel so strongly."
- "This isn't worth getting upset about."
- "It's not worth discussing this problem. He (or she) wouldn't understand anyway."

Over time we adapt to a family environment that makes emotional openness unsafe and we reinforce thoughts supporting the suppression of feelings. The result is, we close down. We lose touch with our real thoughts and feelings. We disconnect from our inner self and become a kind of emotional automaton if the negative process is complete. Consequently, when we grow into adults we cannot be sure what we really think or feel, much less express emotions or controversial thoughts directly.

The process of shutting down is experienced by all of us to some degree, depending on the emotional atmosphere of our childhood household and the sensitivity of our temperament.

For children from disturbed homes who are naturally sensitive, the emotional fallout can even lead to the creation of a false self. That is, when the ability to trust is assaulted, people can build their entire existence around a false self to gain the reassurance and security they crave. A mask of safety shields them from others.

In these instances, people become what psychoanalyst Leslie Farber describes as doubly damaged. First, they suffer from the pain of possessing a "secret, unloving, illegitimate self" that is hidden under the mask. Second, they suffer from "the spiritual burden of not appearing as the person he 'is', or not 'being' the person he appears to be." In effect, such people are living a lie and know it. And they struggle with the chronic fear of being exposed.

Certainly all of us at times will put on an act when we want to impress, please, or placate someone. To some degree, we are all deceptive in everyday interactions where we want to look better, spare someone pain, or make someone feel good. But growing up with serious affronts to our ability to trust can trigger more than the occasional, socially acceptable deception. Sociologist Erving Goffman points out that we are all actors on a stage that includes both public and behind-the-scenes images. If taken to the extreme, putting on an act may break the link between the self we are and the self we display. The result may be a loss of "real self" altogether.

That extreme was caricatured in the movie *Zelig,* in which the protagonist portrayed by Woody Allen is a man with so little sense of self that he turns into whomever he is with. So eager to belong, Leonard Zelig turns black when with a black man, Chinese with a Chinese man, obese with a man who is morbidly overweight. He adopts not only the physical but mental characteristics of members of that group.

People whose link to their real self has broken have what British psychiatric pediatrician D. W. Winnicott calls "false-self personalities." Psychoanalyst Helene Deutsch calls them "as-if personalities." Clinically, they are classed as "borderline personality disorders," since they border on slipping from one personality to another and losing touch with the borders of reality. Regardless of what the disorder is called, at its root is that those people took a serious hit to their sense of trust and were damaged as a result.

When Openness Goes Too Far and Breeds Mistrust

While Richard's parents were described as closed and passively hostile and Marsha's as open and direct, not all open expression by parents promotes trust. Directness, as well, is not always good. Openness needs to be tempered by judgment and respect for others. Otherwise, being too open can be detrimental, much like the too frank person can be rude and damaging.

A classic example of openness gone astray is the couple in the film *Who's Afraid of Virginia Woolf?* The spouses (played by Elizabeth Taylor and Richard Burton) hurl angry taunts to each other. Eventually they bring up the ghost of a dead child that proves devastating and destroys their game-playing with barbs of caustic wit. Similarly, parents who engage in such abuse in front of their children are creating anxiety about relationships. Children see a relationship full of tension that can at any moment spin out of control.

What's more, at times the issues are inappropriate for young children to hear, such as the promiscuity of an older sibling or concern about gambling debts. Parents may think they are being "open with their children." In fact, they are damaging their children's ability to trust, because the young ones simply don't understand the problem and why it is of such concern. What registers in a heated exchange is the anger and tension, which makes them fearful or anxious.

Another way in which openness can diminish trust is when a parent shares harsh judgments about the other parent. For example, some parents during a messy divorce engage in a hostile game of *Put Down the Other Parent*.

Margaret experienced both the tense arguments and the destructive comments by one parent about the other. Though Margaret was by now thirty-three, her experience at twelve contributed to her difficulties with trust and led to divorce. As Margaret explained:

My parents were always fighting when they were together. They fought over the most ridiculous things, like who was supposed to go to the store to get some milk. Sometimes, when they were both home and fighting, I'd go to a friend's house just to get some peace and quiet.

Then, one Saturday afternoon which I'll never forget, my mother suggested we take a ride to the beach. Just her and me. When we got there, after we walked around a little, we sat down and Mother said she had something very important to tell me. She then began to tell me about my father. She told me how he was always running around with other women and was immoral. She said she didn't trust anything he said, that he lied all the time. She confided that she tried very hard to be a good wife and a good mother, but my father made things very hard for her.

She wanted me to understand and side with her, I guess. But I was so embarrassed and uncomfortable. I didn't know what to say. I felt like I was being pulled into a war between the two of them.

I didn't say anything to my father, because I felt so upset and confused about what my mother said. And then a couple of days later, my father took me aside in the living room when my mother was out. When he started to talk, he said the same kind of negative things about her. He said he tried to make a good home for my mother and me but my mother was insecure about herself, and so she had to go out and prove herself with other men.

His remarks left me feeling shattered. I was disgusted by what they both said about each other. I felt I couldn't trust either of them and felt so alone.

As a result, I left home at eighteen to get married. I wanted to get married to get out of the house, but it was a disaster. I was always scared when my husband would want to do anything without me, even just going out to play ball with the guys. I was afraid he'd get involved with someone else, just like my father had done. So I didn't trust him, and I made such an issue of it, that he finally did find someone else. So my worst nightmare came true and we got divorced.

Since then, I've been single for eight years, and it's been very difficult for me. I have trouble with any relationship. Trusting another man frightens me to death, because I worry he'll betray me. And I'm equally afraid to trust myself. It's so difficult for me to make a commitment to anyone, because I'm so confused.

Margaret's inability to trust her parents and their relationship led her into difficulties trusting men, and trusting in her own judgment. Self-trust and trust in others became casualties of her upbringing.

After her husband left, Margaret found herself drawn quickly and indiscriminately into relationships. She felt so deprived of love and intimacy that she grabbed onto whatever pseudo-nurturing came along. This was a prescription for disaster. However, with therapy she came to realize what she was doing. She resolved not to date again until she was more sure that she could distinguish the feelings colored by her past from those in response to real and current events.

From Childhood Games to Adult Patterns of Behavior

The ways that trust problems manifest often reflect the strategies we developed as children to protect ourselves in our family. The family environment is like a furnace where we are forged into the kind of person we will grow up to be. It creates a network of lasting emotions, from love, joy, and pride, to jealousy, anxiety, and guilt. Over time, these emotions grow and shrink in response to circumstances, whether or not they are expressed.

We are all shaped by our early experiences, even if we have moved a great distance from our families, whether in time or geographically. When we move away from our family, or when key people have died, we may still be unable to disconnect from their message.

Wherever we are, whoever we have become, we carry with us the blueprint we developed as a child about who we are and how we are supposed to interact with others. For example, if you had untrustworthy parents, you are likely to have decided: "I can't trust anyone." If your parents didn't show you sufficient attention, you may have concluded: "I'm not worth caring about, so it is dangerous to give myself to love, because no one will love me back."

The particular form that mistrust takes can vary widely. It depends on the specific influence of a particular household and the role that other significant figures—peers, close relatives, teachers—played in early development. Here are some common ways mistrust can manifest for adults:

- Some people find being coupled too threatening, since they fear it won't last. So they avoid getting too involved with one person.

- Others discover that a "solution" to being afraid to trust love is to lead a double life. They seek a secure home base with one partner, combined with an emotional divorce. Then they look for an emotional union outside the relationship. They don't put their emotional eggs, so to speak, in one basket. Their security is in one relationship, their emotional feelings in the other. By diluting intimacy, they feel less vulnerable.
- Still other couples, especially when both are damaged, develop a relationship based on an emotional divorce. Sometimes this evolves out of an unspoken agreement; at other times, both may agree to this openly. In either case, the relationship is empty, but the partners gain satisfaction from outside activities. They may engage in frenzied entertaining, extravagant dining out, change their residence frequently, opt for elaborate decorating, even hop from job to job. But underneath the rush of activities is the couple's attempt to fill the void left by a lack of love in the relationship.

Childhood Survival Tactics Collide with Adult Love

Childhood patterns of adapting to a trust-confusing household take an ironic twist in adulthood. The same survival tactics that worked so well to reduce our childhood fears of closeness now interfere with our ability to love. Just as we mistrusted love as children, so we continue to mistrust as adults, using a similar set of ways to protect ourselves, albeit with a new cast of actors replaying past roles.

Such replays can take various forms. One rather dramatic example involved Susan, who, at age nine, had serious colon spasms that caused her severe pain and frequent diarrhea. After her parents attempted all manner of medical intervention without success, her doctor recommended exploratory surgery. Naturally, Susan's parents were frightened by the prospect of surgery and as a "last resort" took her to see a psychologist.

The psychologist soon concluded that her symptoms were related to family problems rather than to physical causes. It seemed that Susan was experiencing anxiety, which was triggering her spasms. But every time it felt that the therapy was coming close to revealing the source of her anxiety, Susan would get sick and nearly die.

After working with the family for a year, a breakthrough occurred when Susan blurted in a session, "I think I should be sick for the rest of my life." Her mother was shocked: "Why in the world would you say something like that?"

Susan's response turned out to be the key to unlocking the solution. She explained: "When I'm sick, the two of you make me feel relaxed, because you don't fight. But when I'm not sick, you both scare me, because you fight."

Her statement was a revelation, and led her parents to make a conscious decision to work on improving their relationship. When the relationship improved, so did Susan's colon problems.

However, that wasn't the end of the story. Many years later, she became engaged to a young man who was often unreliable. Her fiancé used to fail to keep promises. For example, he would say he'd call but wouldn't do so. He would forget plans they had made. Or he would be extravagant, spending more money than they could afford. When he did such things, Susan became anxious and scared, and her spastic colon acted up once again.

Initially Susan wasn't aware of the reasons for the recurrence of her problem. However, shortly after resuming therapy it became clear that her symptoms recalled her childhood fear about her parents' fighting. Her current symptoms were giving a similar message to her partner, telling him, "This is what you'll be causing if I don't feel safe with you because you aren't reliable." For awhile, Susan's health crisis worked, her partner became concerned and more accountable.

However, after a time the strategy began to backfire, since her partner began to resent being responsible for her well-being. He became so angry that at one point he threatened to leave. As he explained: "Her stomach problems seem to occur only at those times when she's upset with me. It's like she's trying to make me feel like a major heel for screwing up. I may not be perfect, but I can't stand having her make me feel that way. It's like emotional blackmail. It has to stop. I will not continue this way. Absolutely not!"

The conviction behind her fiancé's statement shook Susan. It drove home the realization that she risked losing the man she loved if she kept manipulatively using her illness as she had as a child. With therapy she was able to let go of her sickness and assertively address the unreliability that had upset her.

Less dramatically, but still as destructive, Kevin, a thirty-nine-year-old musician, described how as a child he could get what he wanted by playing his parents (neither of whom he trusted) against each other. As an adult, married for eleven years, he did the same thing. He split his allegiance between his wife and children as a way to avoid being close to either. As a result, the marriage teetered near divorce until he recognized and overcame the reasons for his actions. Kevin gave this accounting:

When I was a child, my parents both had a pattern of being very critical and unavailable. When I tried to talk to them, they constantly told me I was a chatterbox, and that children should be seen and not heard. So I felt very rejected and insecure by their attempts to shut me up and push me aside.

As a result, when I really wanted something, I became expert at playing one of my parents off the other. I didn't think they would give me what I wanted otherwise. I lobbied for gifts, privileges, a waived rule, anything I wanted to gain reassurance. I typically began my con by saying: "But Daddy said I could," or "Mommy promised me this." The con worked since my parents were usually at war with each other and both seemed interested in having me as an ally.

I was able to reverse many unfavorable decisions that way. If the parent I first approached refused, I often emphasized my disappointment with a remark like: "You don't love me anymore; I'll go ask Daddy (or Mommy), because he's (she's) nicer." That tug on their heartstrings was often what I needed to get them to go my way.

When I got married, my wife Jan and I argued because she was unhappy that I didn't support her when she asked the kids to do something or wanted to punish them. I countered that she was too strict. But she contended I was more of a friend to them than a parent and this was undermining her in developing their responsibility. We went back and forth over how to raise our kids for several years. Finally at Jan's insistence I agreed to go to a marital therapist.

After we spent the first two visits describing our difficulties, we each met with the therapist alone. And this is where I came to realize that my childhood pattern was at the heart of the disagreements with my wife. I realized I was using the divide–and–conquer strategy that I had used with my parents.

I was being a friend to my kids to gain their allegiance and set them against her, while using my all]iance with my kids to keep me apart from my wife. I was afraid to let her get too close. The therapist suggested that my parents might have indirectly taught me to do this as a strategy to cope with the insecurity I experienced.

When children keep playing destructive games, it is often because their basic trust in their parents' ability to love and care for them has been undermined; they believe they can only get the love and security they crave through manipulation. Although the patterns of our life are determined by many forces, we live today by what we learned as children. Whatever ways we found to cope with breaches of trust may be reshaped and elaborated by later experiences. However, in some form they continue to influence us. Particular strategies may differ from person to person. Tactics may vary from situation to situation. But the basic dynamics are the same. Consider these examples:

- Laura is afraid to get married. Each time her live-apart lover of many years talks about wanting to get closer and marry, she brushes it off. She is still defending herself against a mother who repeatedly violated her privacy in various ways, from listening in on her telephone calls to reading her personal diary. The thought of someone else invading her space—like her snooping mother—makes her cringe, shut down, and push her sweetheart away.
- Eric is afraid to express his real hopes and feelings to his partner. He retreats into a shell. As a child he lived with unhappy, depressed parents. Whenever he tried to speak to them about things that bothered him, they grew even more despondent and ill. Before long Eric shut down and withdrew himself, fearful that his assertiveness would injure or destroy the people he loves.

- Alison is her own person yet unfulfilled. She is afraid to depend on anyone. Her father failed to live up to his promises, whether to take her on a trip or just come home from the office before she went to bed. Disappointed repeatedly, she grew up afraid of depending on any men in her life; she feared they would disappoint her as well.

Of course, people react differently to the experiences of their families. Not everyone will respond in the same way. Nor will the link of a present behavior to an earlier pattern always be apparent.

People with very similar family backgrounds may thus emerge in various ways. Likewise, adults with similar trust issues may have contrasting backgrounds. There are no simple recipes for how a particular mix of childhood ingredients will influence an adult. Each of us is affected not only by nurture, but also by nature. Our genes influence us, along with the experiences from our environment.

Our genes give us tendencies or propensities that shape, and are shaped by, our experiences. Ongoing studies at the National Institutes of Health and those by other researchers have shown that from birth onward, children exhibit clear-cut temperamental differences. As we develop into adults, we act in a similar fashion.

Usually, for example, the child who is inhibited, shy, and reticent around people will continue to display those traits as an adult, while an energetic, assertive child is more likely to become an energetic, assertive adult. Some children by nature experience more emotional distress and feel more insecure, while others are more apt to respond in a placid, quiet way. Children are not born with specific emotional disturbances, such as anxiety or depression. But we can inherit a sensitivity that leaves us more prone to emotional responses.

Temperament colors perception and shapes responses to family conflicts. For instance, an inhibited child who is naturally sensitive may feel that even a mild show of anger between parents means they are enraged at each other. Overreaction may set the stage to be more anxious when the warning signs of another argument appear. The child may also perceive more hostility in the exchange. Feelings of anxiety, insecurity, and mistrust grow over time, making for more fear and mistrust. In contrast, a youngster with a hardier, more outgoing personality may be less aware of and affected by family disruptions. This child continues to trust while the other one might not.

Learning from, and Overcoming, Past Trust Deficits

Many families plant emotional seeds of love, trust, and respect. In other families, as we have seen, parents have plenty of problems of their own and feelings of trust are compromised. Even so, given abundant love and understanding, trust damage will often be small. However, if the people we count on hurt us and are frighteningly unpredictable, most of us will grow up being terrified of intimacy. While the thought may not be consciously stated, it is powerful nonetheless: If you can't trust your parents, whom can you trust?

Even if past relationships have instilled cynicism, it is still possible to develop trust. By understanding how early experiences with parents and key adults influence us, we can overcome the obstacles placed in the way of trust. What's more, we can understand and help our partners overcome their barriers.

We can also become wiser about when to give the intimate gift of our trust to someone who merits it and when to hold back from trusting someone who isn't worthy of this gift. The challenge, of course, is distinguishing the difference, since we live our lives in shades of gray, not in black and white. As a result, the behavior on which we base our judgment may not always be easily interpreted. Here are some suggestions for sorting out trust issues:

Family Legacy

Be aware of how your upbringing has impacted you. Parents create an insecure home environment in two ways. 1) You were abandoned either emotionally or physically, and you grew up chronically anxious or needy. In your adult relationships, you perceive rejection too easily and too often. Your mistrust theme is "People I love will leave me." 2) They abused you, physically or emotionally, and you grew up feeling suspicious, intimidated, humiliated. In your adult relationships, you perceive control and subjugation too easily and too often. Your mistrust theme is "People I love will hurt me."

Present Focus

Most of us direct our energies toward a love partner's shortcomings. More productively, we can work to overcome our own barriers to trust by reducing the freight of bias and fear we bring from our childhood. To the extent we succeed, we can be more objective and make better decisions about whether to trust or not.

In contrast, if we actively carry the unhealed trust wounds of childhood, we are likely to set ourselves up for repeating the sense of betrayal and disappointment we experienced as children. Either we will choose poorly—seeking out a love partner who is not trustworthy—or we will choose well but interpret our partner's actions negatively, confirming our instinct to protect ourselves. We start with the premise of "guilty until proven innocent."

Wanting our partner to prove lack of guilt places a heavy and unfair burden on the relationship. It puts our partner on the defensive, creating a confrontation where none need exist. And also we often look for proof to support our assumptions. Expectations may even lead our partner to step into the role. (This is like a teacher who expects students to perform poorly and so they do, whereas a positive view will more likely influence the students to do well.) If we expect our partner to be self-centered and unresponsive, for example, we will often find our expectations fulfilled, whether we simply see more of this behavior or our partner conforms to our view.

Stay Here

To counter a tendency to view your partner's actions cynically or interpret behavior in a harsh and unrealistic way, be alert to what triggers your insecurities. To do so, consider the following:

- Focus on your partner's actual behavior in the here and now, rather than jumping to suspicious conclusions about your partner's "real" motives and character.
- Notice your partner's positive behavior and show your appreciation for this.

Come What May

Trusting others is enhanced to the degree that we can trust ourselves to manage whatever vulnerability may bring. Are we willing to deal with the feelings that arise in intimate relations? Acting on the assumption that we are able to face and handle conflict is empowering. What enables us to be emotionally available is knowing that we can be a caretaker for our own hurt or sorrow, that we can comfort ourself in hard times. This allows us to give others a chance.

The Big Gamble

To believe in someone, especially when there is some reason for doubt, means leaving yourself open to hurt and disappointment. What if you avoid reverting to a familiar, self-protective stance and instead risk openly sharing how you feel about a particular event or conflict? You may get hurt, but there is also the chance to strengthen intimacy.

The dilemma is as follows: To be able to trust, we must be willing to take a risk. Some degree of faith is necessary. If we decide to focus on the positive and caring aspects of a partner, we risk being mistaken; if we don't take the chance, we may never find love.

In essence, the key to overcoming the ghosts of the past is to allow ourselves to trust by giving our partner credit for positive behaviors. At the same time, our partner's fallibility must be taken into account, as occasional falls from grace are part of life. Indeed, we should offer support and understanding since our partner may be struggling with some of the same issues we are. Our sweetheart is acting this way not to do something *to* us, though we may perceive it that way. Rather, it is an effort, perhaps misguided, to avoid being hurt.

It is best to give our partner the benefit of the doubt when we first have problems centered on trust, since this approach is based on a love-promoting principle—one that most of us would like our partners to apply to us. Only after we have seen clear evidence that our partner really can't be trusted should we retreat and protect ourselves.

Some people have provocative family histories, including alcoholism, physical abuse, and sexual boundary violations. This may have led to a pattern of poor love choices and repeated betrayals. If so, and you question your ability to judge trustworthiness, seeking the assistance of a therapist is a wise move.

THE LONG 4 GOOD-BYE

WHEN PAST RELATIONSHIPS DAMAGE TRUST

What Happened?

The scene is an exclusive seaside restaurant. A couple in their mid-forties is having dinner. Michael is fit and prosperous-looking. Linda, a former model, now a Ph.D. candidate in sociology, has bright green eyes and a lightly freckled face under a fluff of reddish brown hair. Michael and Linda have been married eighteen years. They are aware of each other, but only vaguely.

This night, as on many others, their attention is directed elsewhere. Presently their eyes and ears are trained on a younger couple seated nearby, a man and woman locked in each other's gaze, speaking softly, inaudibly, sometimes laughing together, other times looking very serious, playful, and earnest, all the while holding hands.

Michael and Linda, disconnected for many years, share a silent thought: Were we ever like that? If we were, what happened? When did the bottom fall out? The bottom, of course, did not suddenly fall out. Relationships do not abruptly collapse. Linda and Michael once thought they had it made. But they failed or refused to recognize the signals, flashing over nearly two decades, that they hadn't. They were divorced shortly after their twentieth anniversary.

The Beginning of the End

Couples often join together inflamed with passion and goodwill; they develop a relationship hoping that their fantasies of "ever after" will spring to life. This is the beginning, the period of courtship and intensity. For some lucky lovers, their hopes are realized. For many others, a few years or even months later, passion and love have been transformed into mutual avoidance, disappointment, hurt, and resentment.

With one in two marriages ending in divorce and countless other relationships existing more out of habit than love, trusting someone to be committed over the long haul is increasingly difficult. In *A Farewell to Arms* Hemingway wrote, "The world breaks everyone, and afterward many are strong at the broken places." True for some, but there is no shortage of people who remain broken.

For most of us, the cost of breaking up is high. Whether formalized by marriage or not, love relations range from those with low emotional involvement to those that in seriousness and intensity are true love affairs. Just so, the implications and consequences of uncoupling also vary. In general, high emotional involvement is matched by corresponding vulnerability. Separation is particularly hard on these former lovers. They find it especially difficult to restore confidence, to build trust, to acquire the conviction that they will—and deserve to—sometime in the future, find someone to give their love, who will reciprocate.

Of course, heartbreak is never easy, regardless of the strength of the broken love. However, when a formerly intense love relationship falls apart, aside from the sadness and mourning that take place, trust has almost surely been a serious casualty.

Indeed, as Diane Vaughan suggests in her 1986 book, *Uncoupling,* dissolution begins with a secret that breaches trust. One of the partners starts to feel uneasy about the relationship. The "we" that the two of them have constructed no longer feels right. At first maybe these disquieting feelings get dismissed as stemming from other sources, perhaps work stress or financial pressures or the emotional valley that everybody goes through. But if it lingers, grows stronger, or fades for awhile only to return, if it takes the form of disenchantment beyond the fleeting anger or disappointment that is common to all relationships, it becomes difficult to express.

Here's how Marion, an attorney, who is now divorced, described her experience:

> It's been four years since Bob and I separated and I still cannot be very exact about when an awareness of trouble began in the marriage. It was very subtle, like there had been a barely perceptible eroding of the foundation, weakening my commitment in innocent increments. I began feeling like I wanted to be away from Bob more than I felt like being with him.
>
> At first I figured it was just overwork and I cut back. But that didn't really help. I couldn't pin my dissatisfaction on something. I complained about a bunch of things but in my heart I knew that wasn't it.
>
> I knew that if I were in love with somebody, the things I complained about wouldn't be a problem. I knew that, but I was frightened to admit it to myself. The implications weren't good. For about two years I just stumbled along, there were no major confrontations between us, but I wasn't happy. I started more seriously thinking about leaving.
>
> All this time Bob didn't really know the degree of my unhappiness; he thought I was just sounding off in an ordinary way. He's a good guy. I can't say he abused me or that he even did anything really bad. How do you tell him you've just fallen out of love?

Not only is the secret difficult to discuss with a partner, it is often a source of discomfort, fear, and confusion for the secret-keeper. As with Marion, it may surface gradually and indirectly through irritation and withdrawal. Or sometimes it appears through a dramatic betrayal such as an affair. In the beginning, though, uncoupling occurs in a subtle, private manner. It is an unexpressed feeling growing in the psyche of a disgruntled lover like a deadly cancer. And by the simple act of walking around harboring and mulling over unhappiness, the secret-keeper inadvertently creates a breach of trust, withholding vital information about the relationship. By being excluded, the other partner is prevented from understanding and responding to a threatening situation.

The secret-keeper may be emotionally discomforted but he or she holds an advantage: plans are often made and carried out without being opened for inspection by the other partner; affection may be expressed that gives a false impression; clandestine support may be sought with a trusted ally. The breach is usually deepened as discontent begins to surface indirectly, through the words and deeds of everyday life: "I wish you would start being on time"; "I can't stand it when you speak with food in your mouth"; "How can you sit around all day and not be productive!" The focus is on the other person's daily failings; the complaints are real but miss the degree of discontent.

Usually, the response to the complaints is at the level at which they were issued—minor grumbles are matched with grumble-like retorts. And so the deception, a deception of true feelings, continues to mask the underlying schism.

Even at the point of separation, both partners are often unclear as to the real basis of their split. In a significant and complex love relationship, it may be years before the emotional puzzle of their lives together is sorted out, if ever. Bob, Marion's husband, still does not understand what happened:

> When Marion told me that she wanted a separation, it was like a death notice. I was stunned. I think I went into shock. I sensed that she had been acting . . . differently. Nothing I could really put my finger on, but it didn't really bother me. I thought it was just part of the everyday stuff that goes on with people living together.
>
> I adored Marion, I never thought . . . I thought we had so much going for us and then I was hit with the hideous realization that the person I thought I was married to wasn't the person I was really married to at all. Did I not do my share of the house upkeep? Did I snore? Was it that I hadn't made my first million? What was it? Sure, Marion had a litany of complaints but frankly I don't believe it. I think she was just disillusioned and she herself doesn't know why. I don't. I still don't. I don't have a clue!

Questioning Your Judgment

As life marches on for the partner who was not privy to the underlying discontent, some questions are carried forward to new relationships: How could I have been so oblivious? How could I have missed the cues? Was he (she) just a good actor? Was all our time together a fraud? Will I think things are well again, only to find they are not? Is it something about me? And (since it's the sense of continuity and permanence provided by commitment that creates an atmosphere in which trust can flourish) the biggest doubt of all: will I ever be able to give myself fully again?

For the initiator of the breakup, those and other questions may also spring up: What went wrong and how do I know that it won't happen again? Now that I have seen how deceptive reality can be—from my former partner's perspective, love seeming to flourish when it did not—will I find myself on the receiving end of an eroded love relationship and not know it? Am I capable of staying in love?

Because a love relationship is the repository of all forms of human emotion, it's easy to understand why its disintegration causes so much stress and anguish. After all, what other adult relationship begins with undistilled and uncritical love—with mutual acceptance—and so often ends in the total negation of a partner through rejection? A formal divorce process (with division of property and assets, child support, and custody) only serves to deepen the wound.

To make matters worse, the breakup rate among couples and the sting of personal experience aren't the only signs flashing 'danger.' Once the seeds of doubt have been planted, we notice more than ever the novels and films about fatal attractions and dangerous liaisons, television shows that make plotting the death of one's partner seem almost routine, and gossip sheets that document every affair, rift, and rupture among celebrities. Initially, at least, the inclination is to circle the wagons and expect the worst.

The Past Revisited

Not only do our experience with the end of love and the media blitz influence our future trust capacity. Nor does it depend solely on how intensely we trusted our most recent partner. It depends also partly on our inner strengths and outer supports. And it will surely depend on our history.

Especially pertinent is our history of love and loss. We've already looked at the toll taken by family conflicts and disturbance; the effects on trust can be devastating. Some of us may not have the resources, either inner or outer, to deal with these experiences. Thus we carry complicating trust issues into adult relationships. Separation, however, is a loss *process;* no wonder that latent childhood losses are likely to burst into the present, adding to the already overwhelming coping process. Here is how Reuben, an editor for a major book publisher, described his experience:

> *When my wife left, I felt as if I was internally unraveling. The turmoil I experienced was analogous to a hurricane that took up residence within me. I couldn't shake the feeling of being a helpless, abandoned child. I believed I would never come out of the fear that encased me. I was emotionally paralyzed. And the really crazy thing was that I wanted the split. I didn't want to remain married to her. I encouraged the separation!*
>
> *About three months later, when I had a little more control, I remembered that as a child I had a congenital lung impairment repaired; my mother then left me in the hospital in a private room in the winter.*
>
> *This picture came to me of the huge hospital building—the gray, dreary room—and it getting dark every night at five o'clock, when the shadows came across my bed and my mother would put on her coat and say, "Good-bye," and I wouldn't see her again until the next day.*
>
> *And one day she didn't show up. She had an accident that evening and was hospitalized herself. In the confusion, no one told me. She just wasn't there. That feeling of panic and abandonment is what came back in spades—when my wife left. I was that little boy again—confused, frightened, feeling helpless and very, very vulnerable.*

And how will this man move on to new relationships? Perhaps, despite his fear and the early scarring that he carries, he will be more successful than would appear. He has the advantage of acknowledging his feelings and the further advantage of understanding the source of his feelings.

In contrast, many men, conditioned to be strong and stoic, do not permit a feeling of bereavement when a loss occurs. Instead, they convince themselves that they are coping magnificently, shedding no tears and carrying on as if nothing disruptive has happened. They are only deceiving themselves into thinking they are "taking it very well," for, in actual fact, they cannot take it. Yes, they may move onto other relationships—but with the closed heart that makes intimacy so difficult and an underlying trust problem so obvious.

Grown-up love is predicated on being able to trust in your own feelings and strength, as well as your partner's. While the premise of immature love is "I love you because I need you," mature love is guided by "I need you because I love you." A temporary childhood abandonment, as we saw with Reuben, can be provocative at the time of a separation, raising the need for security over that of mature love.

If so, then what is the impact when the person you adored and depended upon *never* returned to hold and comfort you? Nina, a thirty-four-year-old single woman employed in pharmaceutical sales, put it this way:

> *My father died when I was nine. Everything changed when I lost him. My mother and my aunt seemed to be in competition for who grieved the most. And being a child, I was never granted the status of a mourner. The world became eternally divided into a "before" and "after."*
>
> *In my thirties, I am still fearful of attaching myself to men. My relationships are purposely shallow. I am flirtatious, engaging, but I don't risk anything. How much bull can I dish and still hold onto this guy? That's the question that comes up for me. When a breakup occurs, I rationalize: I'll live by myself. I'll be self-sufficient. I'll have no accountability, make all my own decisions.*
>
> *And, having made that decision, I then find myself scared to death of being alone. I beg for another chance, not to restore love but to banish the feeling of abandonment I have. I feel: "Don't leave me. I may not be able to make it on my own." I feel: "Help!" It's the same feeling*

I remember so vividly experiencing when my father died. "No, please, don't leave."

Getting Over It

Is everyone who loses a parent in early childhood doomed to guarded vulnerability and compromised intimacy forever? Do all major childhood losses result in trust problems in adult life? The answer is certainly no; however, many studies do indicate that the risk is higher.

In childhood, as in everything else, those whose inner and outer resources are richer have an advantage. Consequently, those children who are temperamentally sturdy are likely to be sturdy in the face of loss. But even the less advantaged, the more fragile child, may be helped by an empathic adult to adapt to the loss by means of constructive mourning.

This is not a point without a degree of controversy, however. Some social scientists take the position that no young child has the capacity to mourn to completion. Consequently, serious attachment and trust problems in adulthood are inevitable. Others disagree (the famed British psychoanalyst and researcher, John Bowlby, among them), suggesting that a strong family unit before the loss, a reliable, comforting caretaker after the loss, and accurate information about the death will promote healing.

For some children, even under the best of conditions, a legacy of the loss may be carried into adulthood, making it more difficult to trust a love relationship. But further resolution may be made possible with the assistance of a trained professional.

Losing a parent by death is a tragedy that can exert a strong presence in intimate relationships. But, another "death," called divorce, impacts us as well. Psychologist Judith Wallerstein and writer Sandra Blakeslee, in the well-regarded book *Second Chances: Men, Women and Children a Decade After Divorce*, contend that society underappreciates the trust damage that takes place in the children of divorce. "They're so scared of abandonment or betrayal that they pick men they're sure of not losing or don't care about losing," Wallerstein says of the daughters of divorce she observed for ten years as part of her landmark study.

Sons of divorce fare no better, according to Wallerstein. She found that many of them bury the feelings that flow from their parents' divorce and constrict emotionally. As a result, they tend to lead lonely, insular lives and are highly sensitive to separation and rejection. Guarding against loss, it isn't unusual for these men to have one foot out the door, literally or figuratively.

William was living with a woman in a tumultuous relationship for three years. He shared this experience:

> *Each time we fought, which was often, I'd run. My parting words were something like, "I can't take this anymore, you're making me nuts, we don't belong together . . ." I stopped short of saying "Let's split" since it wasn't what I really wanted; I really wanted a relationship with Bobbi that worked. Yet each time something came up between us, the same thought ran through my head: "Willy, maybe this lady isn't for you, maybe no one is, maybe you should be alone."*
>
> *I was so scared of it not working, as if my parents' divorce was a legacy of some kind, that I was fated to carry on, that I pushed it to the edge a lot of the time. Lots of testing. I set up all kinds of clever tests and obstacles for Bobbi to overcome. I was trying to prove something but I couldn't really figure out what it was.*
>
> *I think I was extremely fortunate that she is a very dedicated, persevering type person. I pushed her to the edge but she wouldn't leave me; she was firmly committed to working things out. If I had connected with someone else, someone just like Bobbi but not willing to stick with me, it would have never lasted.*

Eventually, Bobbi's commitment led both of them into therapy, where they discovered that William's reaction to conflict was caused by a fear of abandonment. At the time of the argument he felt frightened, anticipating that Bobbi would desert him. The feeling state was reminiscent of his father leaving and his mother being too distraught to properly care for him as a ten-year-old. He couldn't trust the experience enough to expose his vulnerability so he acted angry and brazen while he actually felt insecure and unsafe. In an effort to control the distress and uncertainty he felt, he struck first with his vague threat.

Presently William is able to see a fight as a *disagreement* that's going to end, instead of a *relationship* that's going to end.

Trust Games

Because nobody emerges unscathed from childhood or from adult love relations, none of us is completely trusting, or completely trustworthy for that matter. However, in the weeks and months following a breakup, we are likely to be the most guarded.

Circling the Wagons

Both trusting in oneself and the willingness to trust intimately require time and special consideration in order to heal. We know many new things: how many ways exist for disagreement, that love can fade, that our individual lifestyles will be uncovered for close scrutiny, that sensitive differences must be confronted and resolved. Combined with all this is the lingering memory of a failed relationship that left a painful trail of deception, cover-up, and confusion in its wake.

Often the breakup is difficult and many of us have a history that is highly sensitive to loss. If so, we may carry with us for a long time the separation experience and our responses to it. Expecting to be betrayed, we may seize on every flaw and lapse of a new love: "You see—I should have known I couldn't trust you."

Expecting to be refused, we may not make requests. Or, in contrast, we make excessive demands, furious in advance that they will not be met. Expecting to be disappointed, we are alert to any falter in our partner's enthusiasm, and then a cynic-confirming experience is not uncommon.

We bring about what we fear—driving away prospective lovers by strategies designed, sometimes unknowingly, to defend us against the pain of another loss. Emotional detachment is one such defense. I can't "lose someone I care for" if I don't care. Some of us move into a new relationship asking and giving little, investing almost nothing. We go through the motions, but we have become detached, like a rock, because a "rock," as Paul Simon suggested, "feels no pain. And an island never cries."

Another defense against having our trust breached is to absorb ourselves in the other person's vulnerability without quite exposing our own. We become rescuers. Instead of dealing with our own bruised feelings, we help those who hurt. And through our involvement with another's difficulties we hope to remain in a "one-up" position, protected against our own emotional wounds lurking below the surface. Ironically, such a rescuer often comes to feel used and unappreciated, which is what they were presumably trying to avoid.

Yet another reaction is a premature dive into another relationship—or a series of them. Some of the newly separated initiate brief sexual affairs that reflect complex feelings: a hope of gaining (or avoiding) a new love, an intense desire to stop the pain of loss, and a wish to feel worthy and attractive. In contrast, a few people withdraw from social contact altogether, giving up on ever being able to trust again.

Manipulations also serve to protect a fragile sense of trust. Some men and women choose married people to assure themselves of limited involvement. Others warn their prospective partners not to expect commitment. Some men do so by telling prospects that they consider themselves "free spirits." Some women do so by always being "busy" if too much interest is shown. For many, limiting the amount of time they spend with any one person is the strategy of choice. Even if they reveal their innermost feelings and are inviting, they do so in a controlled manner, arranging not to see the person again for several weeks after each disclosure.

Avoiding emotional intimacy, or seeking it in limited doses, is not necessarily unhealthy. For most people it is part of the healing process. For some, especially those whose history is reactive to loss, it is essential. However, if trust is in need of repair, some solutions are better than others. In fact, certain solutions, such as getting involved with someone who is married, only complicate things.

Hiding Behind a Mask

Sometimes the fear of trusting results in the formation of a false front, a role to avoid being known. Justifying the role is a belief, unconscious or implicit, that to be one's real self is dangerous, that exposure of real feelings will lead to further loss. Thus, there are the Judges, who adopt a critical attitude toward others, rejecting them before they are rejected. Nice Guys, in contrast, become chameleons so as to stave off rejection, convincing themselves to be whatever their new partner wants. To avoid rejection, Conquerors bail out by losing interest just when a relationship turns serious. And Chauvinists take a stereotyped, politicized stance to simplistically explain past and future relationship losses.

Other false fronts to choose from include the Suffering Stoic, the Wounded Idealist, the Witty Comic, the Innocent Victim, and the Rueful Sinner. Whether people conceal themselves in this manner or behind banter, name dropping, or business talk, the result is the same. All facades are cover-ups for the fear of being vulnerable to hurt. Hence they defeat the possibility of a new, lasting love relationship.

All facades share an element of inauthenticity and a hidden trust problem. It is only natural to want to be protective after a loss; "wearing a disguise," however, inhibits intimacy and results in self-alienation.

The path of building trust and enjoying love and intimacy is paved by our willingness to forgo our usual efforts to control things. If we are stuck in false behavior as an ongoing pattern we may go to social events, meet a great many people, and even have numerous affairs, but essentially we remain unrevealed, and hence unconnected.

A New Commitment

When a limb has been broken, the bone needs a period of knitting during which protection is required. If the limb is to grow strong again, however, it must be tested. Our willingness and ability to trust works the same way: We need to try out our healing trust, to exercise our faith in another love relationship, cautiously at first, in order that it may return, in time, to full functioning.

Of course, just as the first steps a patient takes after a long illness may be shaky, the initial experience with intimacy can be unsettling. Yet, despite the grim effects of a breakup, and the fear of trusting again, for most people a dream soon forms of a new life, a new partner: "There must be someone out there who will appreciate and understand me, whom I can trust to love and whose love I can trust."

Jerry has had such a dream. A resident of a small Midwestern suburb, Jerry is unique—as is every person—yet much like other people in seeking to reduce the impersonality of his life. As many do, he chose marriage as his antidote.

Shy and inhibited in his teens, Jerry had few sexual experiences and no real romances until his senior year in high school; then he met Patty, fell in love with her, and thereafter saw her exclusively. He and Patty were married in their early twenties, shortly after Jerry had graduated from a two-year technical college.

Jerry, now thirty-six, and Patty, now thirty-four, are divorced.

Nearly two years have passed since this painful event. Jerry recalls his wounds and his struggle during that period:

> When I married, I was too young. The whole situation was more comic than real, a film in which the action was happening to other people. Neither of us knew what the world was about; we were oblivious to the emotional responsibilities of a committed relationship.
>
> Patty was running away from a mother who was alcoholic; I was over-eager to grow up—to be a man. Marriage, to me, was an almost automatic act, the thing I was supposed to do as part of the "rites of passage." Despite it seeming like a thoughtless decision, I was crazy about Patty, she was my dream girl, I felt very attached to her.

Jerry professed to be deeply connected to Patty. Yet as they passed into adulthood together, their interests, goals, and life views grew far apart. Patty's energies were directed to the raising of their two children, while Jerry approached his work single-mindedly. Commitment to the relationship steadily weakened, and an increasing emotional distance resided between them.

Patty was the first to express serious unhappiness; and when Jerry's response was less than satisfactory, it was she who contacted a lawyer. For six months they lived together while the divorce process wreaked emotional havoc on both of them.

Secret meetings with their attorneys, muffled conversations with supporters, recriminations traded during the adversarial settlement process, and the suspicion each had that the other was out to "screw" them, took a huge toll. The divorce came after thirteen years of marriage and left each mistrusting the other; theirs, as is commonly the case, was a mistrust that generalized to potential new partners.

One said, "All men are shits," and the other said, "All women are out to take you." And neither of them fared well with new relationships for a long while.

Jerry continues:

For nearly a year I didn't date at all. Then I started to venture out, but I dated a variety of women and kept it from getting intense. This satisfied me for awhile, but by the midpoint of the second year I wanted a longer-lasting, more meaningful relationship. The stereotyped image of the carefree single life did not hold up for me. Life as a single in the age of HIV infection isn't real carefree. But the divorce set into motion all kinds of fears about getting close and being hurt again.

Worst of all, I realized that I was at least equally responsible for my marriage failing—perhaps more so. As a result, I lost confidence. Could I trust myself? Trusting someone else, after all, exists only to the extent that I am willing to trust myself, to risk the emotional exposure necessary for closeness.

Right now I am seeing someone special, but I'm cautious. I started therapy and have learned to fight my workaholic tendencies. As obvious as it may seem to somebody else, I'm just realizing that time spent with a woman is as important to her as my financial success. Being emotionally available is my biggest challenge.

When I'm in a positive frame of mind, I remind myself that I was hurt but I survived it. I'm older and wiser. If I find myself doing a secret little "trust test" with my new friend, I talk about it. If there's a problem, I don't hold back and neither does she. This, to me, is how to rebuild trust—act promptly if it seems in danger. Hiding the feeling is the kiss of death.

Patty, Jerry's former wife, has also moved on with her life. She had this to say:

After the initial anger subsided, I became frightened. I berated myself: Why wasn't I able to anticipate the problems? Do I have a blind spot so that this will happen again and again? Then I stopped blaming and began to see the divorce as an opportunity to learn something about myself.

I've done a lot of reading and reflecting in the past two years, and I've come to realize that I probably demanded more from Jerry than he was able to give—and his response was to back up even further. I wanted him to be available, unlike my father, and ironically he turned out to be just like him.

*Right now I'm just dating, nothing serious. My most important les-
son has been that I thought I was marrying a man different from my
father but unconsciously I was drawn to what was familiar, hoping to
achieve a different outcome. I don't want to do that again!*

Although there is not a guaranteed ready formula for repairing trust
and moving on after a breakup, some guidelines do apply:

- As Patty suggests, we tend to return to the familiar in a new
  relationship. We feel impelled to transfer unhealed childhood
  wounds onto the present. Choosing a person who fits our
  drama, we tend to act out the same old tragedy. In so doing, we
  damage our trust of others and ourselves still further—unless
  awareness and accompanying behavior intervene. If you are not
  sure how your childhood affects your mate selection and your
  ability to trust, seek professional assistance. It will help ready
  you for intimacy.

- Coming into a relationship with the hidden expectation that
  it is your new lover's responsibility to mend your past wounds
  is bound to leave you feeling betrayed. The tendency to lump
  all past failed relationships together can also undermine
  future bonding. It leaves you feeling so sensitized to being let
  down that the slightest flaw in your partner can feel like a
  major betrayal.

- Avoid the tendency to idealize a new partner. Women may be
  more prone to this myopia than men, but both sexes tend to do
  this in the so-called honeymoon phase of a relationship. When
  the relationship has settled in, we are bound to get let down
  and feel, "They're all alike and not to be trusted."

- If you have the tendency to fall "head over heels in love," fight
  it. Give yourself time to become known and to know your
  partner, flaws and all, before giving away your heart.

- When feelings of disappointment seep into your mindset, even
  subtle ones, face them rather than stewing about them. Ask
  yourself why you feel let down: "What did I expect that I
  didn't get?" And "Is it realistic to expect it?" The expectations
  that seem reasonable or even marginal to you warrant discussion with your partner. Avoiding the issue is likely to perpetu-
  ate your feelings of mistrust.

- Sharing your feelings on sensitive matters is risky. Bear in mind, however, that your best hope of healing a trust wound with a partner is getting a caring acknowledgment. You risk rejection by being open. But if you have the courage, you will find out where you stand. If your approach emphasizes your feelings rather than an attack on your partner, it is more likely that the response will be receptive.

- Lastly, consider that the more trusting you are, the more likely you are to be trusted by others—a finding that has come out of the research of psychologist Julian Rotter at the University of Connecticut. Dr. Rotter suggests that trust, like many other interpersonal behaviors, tends to be reciprocal; you are more likely to get in return what you are perceived as giving. Especially while you are mending a broken heart, this requires some judgment as to how far to risk your trust.

DANCE-AY LOVERS

THE TRUST-MISTRUST RELATIONSHIP

The Fear of Surrender

Practically all relationships experience trust struggles and conflicts at one time or another. Usually the dispute is less dramatic than a crisis but important nonetheless. Some people, however, find it exceedingly difficult to emotionally commit, because their unresolved trust conflicts are so prominent. Their relationships have mistrust and fear of closeness at their core.

Usually we think of commitment as an issue faced by people contemplating marriage. Yet many people who are already married or in an exclusive relationship never really committed to intimacy. Indeed, mistrustful lovers feel most anxious when they are pressed for emotional closeness.

Intimate relating involves interdependence between partners who maintain their own individuality. Intimacy requires both an *I* and a *We*. Individualism (the *I*) must balance with togetherness (the *We*). A healthy sense of *I* is essential in order to allow for a full expression of *We*. However, for some individuals, such as those whose childhood was marked by an overly controlling parent, a strong sense of identity may not have developed.

Love partners with this type of history—a parent whose life was too enmeshed with every move—often have trouble with boundaries. They draw a broad territorial circle around their emotional lives. Attempts by a partner to promote closeness feel like being invaded. A desire for emotional togetherness is not viewed as reassuring but as a violation of privacy and—sometimes on an unconscious level—as a betrayal. In fear of losing their separateness, they overreact—often with anger or further withdrawal—in an effort to assuage the anxiety triggered by the underlying mistrust of closeness.

One such individual, Carl, is thirty-three and has been married for eight years.

> *When my wife was in her sixth month of pregnancy, it hit me: "I'm stuck; I'm really married." We had been married for several years, but I never felt really connected; emotionally I still considered myself a loner. There were no real responsibilities tying me to Cathy. With a child coming, I felt really scared. Was I doing the right thing? Was marriage really for me?*
>
> *Up until then, I never really had to consider those questions. I guess in the back of my mind I always figured I could get out. With the pregnancy, I saw it was too late. What kind of heel would leave his wife in her sixth month? I couldn't live with that, but I also felt, more than ever, that I was tied down. What a lousy sense of timing. When Cathy flew to Minnesota to visit her aunt, I remember thinking maybe the plane would crash and I'd be free. It was a horrible thought. We were doing a lot of bickering, but I always considered Cathy a friend—a very decent, giving, and accommodating person. I was beside myself.*
>
> *I started avoiding her, even more so than in the past. My activities, and there were plenty—golf, tennis, overtime at work, hanging around with buddies, burying myself in the TV—made the statement, "I am an individual and I don't want to have to answer to anybody; I value my separateness above all." My attitude was unreasonable, but of course I didn't see it then. Any attempt at closeness felt like my head had been put in a vise and was being squeezed. Honestly, at times I felt actual nausea.*
>
> *In retrospect, it seems obvious that I transferred the relationship I had with my mother onto Cathy. My mother was the kind of person who had*

to intrude in every aspect of my life—even to the point of banging on the bathroom door during my teen years and screaming, "What are you doing in there?" If I rebelled from her intrusions, she'd respond with one of her famous phrases: "This is for your own good," "You have to trust my judgment" (rather than your own!), or the real guilt clincher, said with moist eyes, "I'm only doing this because I love you so much." She may have been well intentioned but it took me several years to untangle myself from her controlling grip.

Of course control is not necessarily a dirty word. It is a parent's responsibility to protect a child from the dangers in the world and this requires control. However, as the child evolves and is able to explore the world with reasonable risk, it is also the parent's responsibility to back off, even if uneasily, and allow the child to experience the pleasure of standing alone. For example, a mother who restrains her toddler from climbing up to a hot stovetop we don't consider to be intrusive; we call her prudent. She is exercising control that is in accord with reality, motivated by her child's well-being and safety. But what if that mother is still restraining her child in the same manner ten years later?

Beverly, aged forty-three, the manager of a large travel agency, expressed particularly strong sentiments:

I've worked hard to get where I am, but my mother doesn't think I'm capable of dressing myself. Her whole life has been wrapped up in me. And when I married the first time, in my twenties, it got worse. She didn't let up. She was always bringing food over to our place, offering to help with the finances despite the fact that we were holding our own, and giving unsolicited advice on anything and everything. She would even pull me aside for a "secret" conference to tell me Jimmy wasn't good enough for me—just like every guy I dated before him was never good enough. When I asked her to stop interfering, she'd well up in tears and cry, "What's wrong with a mother looking out for a daughter she loves?"

Jimmy complained all the time that I wasn't there for him, I was too distant because I was so involved with my mother. I would shoot back that our problems had nothing to do with her. We bickered constantly. His parting words to me were that I would never be able to give of myself until I had a self apart from her.

For a long time after we split I was very bitter. Now with the experience of several more failed relationships it pains me to acknowledge that he was right. It's bizarre but I believe that our bickering was my way of creating space in the relationship. Closeness was somehow a threat, maybe a disloyalty to my mother.

For a number of years I really didn't trust that closeness was safe. It felt suffocating and I struggled along never making the connection to my mother—maybe because even the thought of seeing it that way was guilt-provoking. The picture of my mother standing before me with tears running down her face didn't instill courage!

Being Both Separate and Close

Becoming a separate self is not a sudden revelation but an unfolding. It evolves slowly, over time. During the first three years, in predictable stages, we venture upon a journey as important as any we will ever take, the beginning of autonomy and independence. It is during this period that we gain a growing sense of a world existing outside ourselves—a world to be looked at, touched, explored. If as toddlers we had an adult's command of language, we would have said: "There are all kinds of marvels out there to explore, wonders everywhere. I am ready to venture out, off your lap and with my newfound locomotion, survey the sights and experiences."

Inevitably, as children walk, jump, and climb, they fall, bruise, and bleed. Realization comes that there is a price for standing alone. "If I leave Mom's side will I perish?" "Will I be able to return to her comfort again?" Ideally, the mother smiles, encourages exploration, and is there when needed. Children derive from that attitude a growing sense of confidence and a safe feeling about the world.

But what of children who are not encouraged to explore, to master, and to risk failure? Often they feel helpless and stifled. When they wander off Mom's lap to the sound of her insecure voice once again calling out, "Come back, you'll get hurt!" they may dutifully return. However, inside the shell of conformity their inner drive for autonomy is being denied. (A too-involved parent needs a child to remain dependent often as a result of the parent's unresolved fear of abandonment.) Overcontrolled children often become fearful of being separate—and at the same time terrified of being engulfed. On the one hand, they have learned to be frightened of being more independent. On the other, they are overwhelmed by the intensity of their overinvolved parent.

Craving the sweetness of unity yet dreading engulfment makes intimacy both difficult and confusing. Trusting in yourself is frightening when your most basic experience involving the most powerful person in your life suggests that you are not capable. Likewise, to trust the intimate advances of others raises the suspicion that they too will swallow your "I" if you lower your guard. And if you do expose your vulnerability, only to feel pressured as you had anticipated, a deepening mistrust is likely to prevail.

Autonomy faces many challenges throughout life, and some parents never outgrow the need to remain in control of their children. At every stage, growing independence is viewed as a loss that parents fight off.

Adolescence is when children actively confront parental values, tastes, and authority. And in a reasonably healthy family, parents tolerate (and even appreciate) the need for rebellion as a normal stage of emotional development. Insecure parents, however, aren't so understanding. They defend against their anxiety by reinforcing their child's dependence and sabotaging independence. They act as if their child's separate existence is akin to parental homicide. The teenager will often become an adult who has unresolved guilt about separation and in subtle and not-so-subtle ways mistrusts the closeness efforts of anyone, especially in a love relationship. Inside the struggling adult is a frightened child who fears that the experience of closeness will be as it was with mother; he will be trapped in a symbiotic union forever.

Without the child realizing it, this fear of engulfment becomes a core part of adult love relations. In various ways, love is kept at bay because it is experienced as unsafe. Such adults develop into distancers, persons who unconsciously push others away. They keep love partners at a distance with the rationalization that they need space; they dislike accountability; they get tense if they feel pinned down; they are restless and free spirits at heart. The variety of obstacles at distancers' disposal—from avoiding self-disclosure to all manner of betrayals and avoidance strategies—are endless.

In short, residing within distancers' cool exteriors are children who were not allowed to satisfy a natural need for independence. They mistrust anything that hints at restraint.

The Too-Hungry Lover

Too much involvement from a parent can influence the degree of trust we place in others and ourselves. Yet none of us can begin to believe in ourselves without some assistance from our childhood caretakers. All of us need a mother figure who guides us in our efforts to reach out and learn about the world, a mother who assists us to establish a stable sense of security, who reassures us so that we can place trust in our wishes and feelings. As small children we cannot fulfill or even recognize our needs. Our mother helps us recognize our needs and is sympathetic to their fulfillment.

Sometimes the mother falls short; she is emotionally unprepared for the challenge of nurturing a child. In contrast to the controlling, over-involved caretaker, an underinvolved parent is not equipped to meet any needs but her own. Consider a little child whom such a mother pushes away. "I'm busy now," she says. "Later. Go. Don't be a pest." The child refuses and clings. Angrily, she drags the little one, kicking and screaming, out of her room and locks the door. Imagine the child whining through the locked door, pleading and raging for the mother's comfort. This happens not once, not twice, but often. In various ways mother is always too busy. What will this child be doing as an adult? What will such a person be seeking in a love partner?

Very often these children grow up hungry for connection; they seem to have an insatiable need for closeness. They become pursuers, in search of a sense of oneness with another. The children who experienced rejection had believed that if they tried harder their mother would love them. Now as adults they keep alive the fantasy that somewhere there exists a mate who will finally meet all their emotional needs.

Pursuers want to do things together all the time. If a partner wants alone time, or in some way fails to satisfy (as he or she inevitably will) the pursuer feels let down, rejected, and a vague sense of betrayal. Especially when they feel deprived, they crave physical affection and reassurance. Simultaneously however, they often criticize their partner as someone who can't handle closeness. Underneath the clinging behavior is a young child who needed more time on a parent's lap.

In the early days of life, especially, children need lots of contact, caressing, holding, and social stimulation. Abundant evidence exists that without such close contact, physical and psychological development will be impaired. The groundbreaking experiments on infant monkeys conducted by psychologist Harry F. Harlow, published in 1958, states the case dramatically. Briefly, Harlow supplied newborn monkeys with two surrogate mothers fashioned from wire: one warmed with a light bulb and covered with a soft terry cloth, the other merely a bare wire frame. The monkeys were divided into two groups, one given a nonnursing cloth mother, the other given a nursing wire-frame mother.

Harlow observed that monkeys fed from the wire-framed mothers spent only enough time on those wires to stay alive. The rest of the time they spent clinging to the comforting cloth-covered mothers. Harlow wrote, "We were not surprised to discover that contact comfort was an important basic affection or love variable, but we did not expect it to overshadow so completely the variable of nursing . . ."

In essence, Harlow found that his infant monkeys valued warm, soft contact more than they did nourishment, for they preferred to cling to "mothers" who provided physical contact without nourishment to wire ones who did supply nourishment.

Humans are not unlike the primates Harlow studied. The need for attachment is basic and if thwarted, especially in the young and dependent years, it nearly always leads to impairment. For some, particularly if the deprivation was severe, isolation is chosen as a way to avoid further loss. Indeed, it is not uncommon for parental neglect to result in an adult who is distant and guarded.

For others, however, the pursuit of closeness becomes a life theme, in an effort to assuage the anxiety of separateness. We transfer the fear of separation into expectations of our children, friends, business partners and —most intensely—our lovers. Expecting to be abandoned, we hang on for dear life: "Reassure me," we seem to say. "Show me you care. Hold me, accompany me, be with me, now, always."

Viewing anything less than total devotion as rejection, behaviors by a partner that are not inclusive may be challenged as betrayals. "How could you do that to me!" becomes a chronic plea.

Alec and Marie

Alec is a young man whose childhood memories suggest a deprivation that has left him hungry for attachment. He was the youngest of three brothers; by the time he was four, his two brothers had moved out.

When he was six, his mother had "some kind of breakdown." She was never very attentive, Alec contends, but from then on his house was usually dark, with the shades drawn. His mother was often in her robe and she never seemed to talk. His earliest memories of her were with a cup of coffee in one hand, a newspaper spread out in front of her and the television blasting. Her attention alternated between the daily news and the soap operas. She never made breakfast or even got up from in front of the television to see him off to school. When he returned from school, his mother would be in the same position or taking one of her long naps behind a locked door. His father traveled a great deal and seemed to have given up on the family, sleeping in a separate room when he was home.

During adolescence, Alec avoided getting involved with girls. He was a love 'em and leave 'em type of guy. He spent two years in the military, practicing the same pattern of short-term relationships. Secretly he held the dream that one day he would meet someone who would do everything for him, somebody who would fulfill his every need, somebody who would compensate for the neglect he suffered at home. When he met Marie, a soft-spoken and gentle woman, she seemed to be his dream woman incarnated.

Alec and Marie saw each other constantly for three months, fell very much in love, and were married. Without a word of discussion, early in their relationship they set up a pattern of overinvolvement that eventually drove them apart. Throughout their courtship and marriage, Marie stopped seeing her friends; and at Alec's request, they always did things as a couple. He discouraged individual desires. Rather, only those actions that were mutually pleasing were accepted.

In addition, Alec depended on Marie's advice about his career and appearance, and on her views regarding current events. She was his everything. She did his laundry, cooked his meals, and reminded him of important dates. Initially, Marie was flattered by the respect he had for her opinions and viewed their lifestyle as a respite from the hectic social life she formerly led.

During the second year of their relationship, Alec remained content with the togetherness arrangement, but Marie began to feel closed in and wanted more privacy, more time to pursue her interests and increased social contacts. She began to complain to Alec that he depended on her for too much. Alec, resenting Marie's individuality and feeling threatened by it, became very critical of her. He told her that she should view his reliance on her as a compliment and accused her of being cold and rejecting. Marie grew impatient and angry, and started seeing her friends despite Alec's protests.

During the next three years, the struggle escalated. By then, mutual resentment and suspicion had consumed them. There was no real communication, and whatever feelings they once had for each other had been soured by Alec's dependency. They separated after four years of marriage.

The Urge to Merge

Alec's plight is only unusual in its intensity. Deep within all of us—including those who flee from closeness as if it were a deadly virus—lies the wish for perfect, all-encompassing nurturance. Yearning for moments of oneness with another, longing to experience the comforting intimacy of intense love, is entirely human and desirable. But for some, like Alec, whose early need for nurturance was not satisfied, these wishes dominate our love life and cause us to feel mistrust and betrayal each time our partner is less than we demand.

Consider a woman described by analyst Peter Smith. Trying to choose between two attractive marriage proposals, she made her choice while out to dinner with one of her suitors at the moment he scooped up a morsel of food and spooned it—like a mom—into her mouth. She viewed that act as a compelling promise to take care of her in a most basic and complete manner. The decision was made emphatically and instantly. He was her choice.

And how will this woman feel when her husband is not always there to meet her needs? Let down? That hardly captures it. Pierced through the heart is more like it. Dr. Smith suggests that for such people—in contrast to the more conventional desire for closeness—the longing for merging, for oneness, has no boundaries. Instead it sets itself up as a driving force in one's life that is especially prominent in love relations. It gives the phrase "the urge to merge" new (and stronger!) meaning.

The Lovemap of Distancers and Pursuers

The Influence of Gender

The saga of distancers and pursuers exists at many different intensities. Perhaps the most common version is a man as distancer and a woman as pursuer. It would seem that nearly every heterosexual adult with some experience of romance has encountered this theme, at least to some degree. As a group it is apparent that the two sexes travel a different relationship path. In the United States, most researchers concede that boys and girls are brought up in divergent ways, taught different skills, rewarded for diverse acts. Witness some discriminating reactions to male and female children: A shy little girl is considered cute; a shy boy is admonished to act like a man. Girls are allowed comfortably to kiss each other and to cry openly without shame; boys who even touch each other had better be "horsing around," and crying is done only at the expense of ridicule.

These behavioral distinctions, which may seem extreme to some, were confirmed in a study commissioned by the United States government. The majority of tested parents hugged or cuddled their sons after the average age of five less often then they did their daughters, regardless of age. They would not kiss male children at all after a certain age (usually the onset of adolescence), and would discourage boys as young as four years old from sobbing by calling them crybabies or telling them to "act their age." When asked to explain the reason for treating sons and daughters differently, the most common response from parents was: "I don't want my son to grow up to be a sissy."

Is it any wonder that women often complain that their lovers are not expressive and have difficulty exposing vulnerability? Or that men lament that women are asking too much of them?

Psychologist Carol Gilligan highlights another facet of male/female development. Originally, she notes, both sexes were symbiotically merged with mother; a child's first identification was with her. While it is true that both boys and girls must deal with the issues of attachment and autonomy, having a female as the primary caretaker has a different effect on the sexes. For little boys, prolonged symbiosis will threaten their masculinity far more than it threatens the femininity of little girls, who are the same sex as their caretaker.

Thus girls continue their "we" relationship with their mother while boys—in order to be boys—are forging their "I." Boys are distinguishing themselves from the female parent and girls are identifying with her. Boys learn early to separate themselves from women, developing a shield against their strong urges to merge with Mom, a shield that, for some, lasts a lifetime. In contrast, girls are more afraid of separation, for their feminine identity is founded upon their relationship with another female. And so the dynamics of the chase are securely in place.

Many men and women who become partners accommodate the differences in their relationship orientation. Yes, it is a struggle; and sometimes it is an unsuccessful struggle that ends in a breakup. However, gender differences alone (apart from a provocative history in which attachment or autonomy was badly compromised) do not usually create severe, chronic trust problems.

The trust/mistrust relationship is at its height when two provocative histories collide. In these instances, either sex may play either role. Because of social conditioning, males in the pursuer role may *appear* independent while subtly being very demanding. A man can, after all, pursue by an insistence that he be taken care of in conventional ways— cooked for, have his laundry done, have the house cleaned, and his social life organized.

Women in emotional pursuit of a man are more likely to be accepted as normal. However, women whose history left them hungry for attachment possess an intensity that combines forcefully with gender issues. Before long most men are likely to find these women overwhelming.

Pursuers and Distancers Together

While gender plays a role in the pursuer-and-distancer choreography, it is the underlying emotional dynamic that takes center stage. To understand that dynamic, let's first review what we learned about pursuers and distancers earlier in this chapter:

- Pursuers are usually people who grew up with an unsatisfied need for attachment. They react to the fear of abandonment by seeking a high degree of togetherness and dependency in relationships. When their partner does not meet their togetherness and dependency needs, they tend to pursue harder and then may coldly withdraw. Pursuers view their partner's attempts at isolation with suspicion and eventually experience a deep sense of betrayal.

- Distancers are people who have an unsatisfied need for autonomy. They like to view themselves as self-reliant and have difficulty showing their needy, vulnerable, and dependent sides. They too view their partner's behavior with mistrust, sabotaging attempts at closeness or cutting off a relationship entirely if it gets too intense.

Of course, to make the entire matter more interesting, nature and nurture can combine in unpredictable ways. It is not always the child of the overinvolved, controlling parent who becomes a distancer, and it is not always the neglected child whose hunger for attachment leads to lifelong pursuit. Sometimes, perhaps due to a hardy temperament, neither a pursuer nor a distancer arises from what appears to be a fertile field. Other times both characteristics emerge in the same person, and in still other instances the trend is reversed; the neglected child isolates and the controlled child repeats the pattern of control and engulfment.

Nevertheless, distancers and pursuers abound. And like moths to a flame, they often view each other as "everything I ever wanted in a lover." This experience lasts until the passion of their honeymoon period has diminished. Then reality sets in, and an unsettling game of push and pull begins. Each member of the couple monitors the balance of separateness and togetherness, automatically and sometimes unconsciously making moves to restore separateness (when anxiety about autonomy sets in) or togetherness (when anxiety about attachment sets in).

Sometimes this pattern continues through the course of a relationship. Other times, there is a reversal: the partner who usually retreats suddenly moves forward. When this occurs, the partner who typically advances usually moves back, revealing that pursuers at heart also don't trust intimacy. Underneath their hunger is a fear that a love found would be a love lost.

In time, a subtle but potent uneasiness runs under the surface of the relationship. Both partners feel unsafe and resentful. Distancers suspect their partner's warmth, regarding love gestures as manipulations. As one mate said, "Every time she comes on to me I wonder, 'What does she want now?' " The pursuing partner in turn viewed that distancing as an indication that she was not lovable and accused the mate of being involved in an affair. Indeed, several times when he was working late, she hired detectives to confirm his whereabouts.

Pursuer-and-distancer relationships often follow a cyclical pattern. When the waters are calm, their mistrust of each other subsides, but in times of stress, suspicion and mistrust escalate. It may be an illness, a financial worry, a possible career setback, or simply a vague fluctuation in self-esteem that increases a feeling of vulnerability. Whatever the cause, there is now an increased expectation to be understood and gratified. If that response is less than satisfactory—if one partner views the other as withholding or demanding rather than responsive—the feeling is likely to be that he or she is an enemy rather than a friend.

Here is how one couple described their experience. Mary Jane met Timothy at a singles' bar and has been living with him for over a year:

I don't know why I continue the relationship with Tim. He never calls me from work anymore, he comes home looking and acting unfriendly, and he puts on the sports channel before the sound of the door closing behind him has left the room.

It's bad enough that we hardly relate but when my kid sister asked me to accompany her for an abortion, I needed Tim to be there for me. This was something I really needed support for and he became even more remote than usual. He told me I was demanding. Demanding! My kid sister was in trouble and I wanted a shoulder to lean on—is that demanding? I don't feel I can count on Tim and that scares me. That really scares me.

Tim put his version this way:

When we first met, Mary Jane impressed me as kind of laid back and this attracted me. Now she seems to have changed so much. I can never have time to myself. She's always complaining about me; not only does she not let me have my space, her complaints are coupled with a verbal onslaught and sometimes physical abuse.

Honestly, the only time I really feel safe around her is when we're in the company of other people. It's embarrassing to say this but the thought has sometimes occurred to me that Mary Jane could try to kill me in her rage. Yeah, she scares me too.

On the surface, pursuer-and-distancer relationships seem like a sure-fire prescription for aggravation. So why do people fall into them so easily? Is it masochism? Lack of intelligence? Hardly.

The most likely basis for what might seem to be a puzzling attraction is a compulsion to repeat. A psychological concept called *repetition compulsion* suggests that we do again and again what we have done before, in an attempt to replay and then correct an earlier unhappy experience. Although the reenactment of their childhood drama brings pain with it, distancers and pursuers transfer feelings from childhood onto each other in an effort to rewrite the script with a happy ending.

Rapprochement: Breaking the Cycle

Is a happy ending possible, or are distancers and pursuers like proverbial lemmings heading for the cliff? The answer, for those willing to put their efforts into breaking the cycle, favors the possibility of a happier existence. For although we are driven by some forces that are beyond our control and awareness, we are also active authors of our fate. And while it is true that we tend to repeat the patterns established in childhood, we are also capable of shaking up the old arrangements. Here's how to start:

- Become aware of your history and how it has influenced you. You do this through reflection and therapy, and by becoming a more astute observer of your reaction to everyday events. Realize that a kiss is not just a kiss. Rather, the outer event filters through your unique psyche. There it mingles with your biases and predisposition, leaving you to experience it as either sweet intimacy, a meager gesture, or an outrageous intrusion.

- Don't block off the feelings hidden beneath your usual reaction of pursuing or taking flight. Instead, reflect on the feelings of pain, rage, and fear that are hiding beneath these adaptations. As you open to a greater understanding of yourself, you need to risk sharing this with your partner, with the understanding that this sharing is a sacred trust that must not be violated. This means not using a disclosure to shame or chastise a partner, keeping the disclosure confidential. If trust is maintained, you will gradually begin to view your partner's childhood wounds as well as your own with more compassion. (It may seem as if simply talking about your feelings is insufficient. However, the combination of increased awareness and talking out your feelings is truly a dramatic change from the past pattern.)

- While building an atmosphere of safety and trust with your partner, redefine your relationship with your parents. This can be a powerful step toward healing the childhood wounds that still fester. Both distancers and pursuers often find that they have a *reactive* relationship with their parents. People are usually the most reactive when they feel emotionally threatened or provoked. Frequently the feelings that arise are far out of proportion to the events that evoked them. When you are reactive, you say things such as: "Every time my mother offers one of her suggestions I can feel the anger erupting in me." "They really know how to get to me. Just being around them gets me tense." "I can't believe that nothing I do ever gets a positive response from them. I don't know why it still upsets me."

- The opposite of being reactive is being *responsive*. When you are responsive, you are aware of your feelings but don't let them run you. This is extremely empowering. Responsiveness allows you to maintain some control in the face of the thoughts and feelings of your parents as well as your lover. You will open all sorts of new options and choices in your dealings with others, because your perspective and your sense of reason aren't being blurred by emotion. Feeling more in control, you will be in a better position to take control of your love life.

Of course, becoming responsive is easier said than done; behavioral changes are a struggle for everyone. In essence it requires that you identify what it is that you want, believe, or feel—and stay your course. It also involves being open to views that are in conflict with yours, rather than getting defensive. In talking to an intrusive parent, for example, instead of arguing, explaining yourself, or apologizing, you might simply say, "You're entitled to your opinion." If the parent has some advice, you might respond with, "That's interesting," or "Let me think about that," rather than the usual anger reaction.

- It is sometimes helpful to imagine yourself in conversation with a parent and rehearse your responses in advance. This shouldn't be too difficult to do since most of the conversations you have with your parents are probably similar. By now you could easily write the script. Indeed, if you are locked in a distancer-and-pursuer cycle, the same applies to your interaction with your partner. There, too, you can rehearse your reasoned responses in your mind's eye.

In some ways it is easier to change the interaction with a parent who is intrusive than with parents who neglected you (i.e., were inadequate, had overwhelming problems of their own, or for whatever reasons were unavailable). In many cases you may find yourself defending your parents or minimizing their effect on you. (This is especially true of men since, as we have seen, they are conditioned to ignore many of their feelings.)

Talk to your partner about your experience and, perhaps with coaching from a therapist, talk to your parents about your feelings. It is not so important whether your parents are receptive, for you are doing it for yourself. Once you are able to truly see, believe, and connect your feelings to the emotional neglect you experienced, you will be in a better position to rid yourself of the mistrust and fear of closeness that impairs your ability to be loving.

Awareness, a change in attitude, and altered behavior are all necessary ingredients to the change process. The suggestions above are only the beginning; and they're not easy. Fear of change accompanies the desire for a more satisfying love life. But bear in mind that if you are experiencing a strong distancer-and-pursuer pattern in your love relations, it is a signal of unresolved childhood issues—and you are unlikely to become trusting of love without confronting and healing them. Do it for yourself. If you have a partner who will join you in this process, all the better.

JEALOUSY, 6 LOVERS' HELL

Jealousy as a Trust Issue

Jealousy is the reaction we experience when we feel we might lose a love partner to someone else. We feel fear, anxiety, perhaps a diminishing of our worth, and a loss of power and control. After all, someone else may now get what we have, want, or hope to preserve.

We can be jealous about anything—someone getting an object or job we covet, for example. But in relationships, jealousy occurs when someone we love is drawn to another person, or we think he is. We fear losing our lover, being compared to a more attractive rival, our lover spending less time with us, or otherwise being pulled away.

The potential loss triggers other negative emotions, such as fears of being lonely, suffering a loss of face, losing influence over our partner or control over the relationship, and other possible losses.

Jealousy fears are trust issues. Typically we feel jealous because we mistrust our partner's commitment to us. What's more, we have lost trust in our worth when we are jealous of our partner spending time with someone else (even in chatting or cocktail party banter). We start to think we aren't good enough, that someone else is better than us; we feel a loss of personal power; we don't trust ourselves to stay in control.

In the midst of jealousy, we worry that the person we care for will be lost to someone more "deserving" than we are. That makes us question and mistrust our own adequacy; we make the mistake of thinking we must be less deserving if the person we love is less interested in us.

On the Big Screen

A dramatic example of how jealousy can erode a seemingly loving relation—and leave the ruins of trust in its wake—is the motion picture *Eyes Wide Shut* by Stanley Kubrick. This film depicts a highly successful New York physician (Tom Cruise) and his attractive wife (Nicole Kidman).

The unraveling of their relationship starts after a New York cocktail party. The husband notices his wife flirting with an engaging man who proposes a tryst; she declines, explaining, "But I can't. I'm married." Yet she is clearly intrigued, and later, while smoking marijuana before she and her husband go to bed, she confesses an unfulfilled fantasy about a Navy man she met before she was married.

It was just a flirtation and wishful longing that is long over, but it triggers a trust crisis for her husband. He can't put his vision of her making love with another man out of his mind. He is mistrustful of her dalliance with the man at the party, questions the strength of their love, and begins an obsessive journey through New York's sexual underworld to live out his own fantasies. He has several encounters with a prostitute and goes to a medieval-style bacchanal, which looks like something out of Dante's *Inferno,* underlining the loss of control and mistrust of his wife. Though he wears a mask at the party, he doesn't fit in and is exposed—as if he is wearing his lack of trust on his sleeve. He flees, feeling himself in great danger. And he is.

The party and the film are a parable of how jealousy out of control can undermine our trust in everything: our partner, ourselves, the very world we live in. The husband's nightmare ends only when he resolves to reject the growing monster his mistrust has created and reveal his fear and vulnerability to his wife. Their relationship is still shaky but at least, through his revelation and willingness to trust again, he and his wife can begin to heal.

The Continuum of Jealousy

Eyes Wide Shut portrays what can happen at the extreme of intense jealousy. Jealousy actually lies on a continuum. It ranges from apathy, when people don't care what their partner does (generally because they don't feel love or commitment), to the high anxiety and suspicion that breeds a hostile or even lethal reaction.

In the middle are the kind of jealous twinges that most of us experience. It may be annoying or act as a wake-up call to pay more attention to the relationship. Many people don't even think of it as a problem. They may say, "I feel jealous because I love you," or "He shows he's jealous when I'm talking with someone else. That must mean he really cares."

Often people joke about small displays of jealousy. They may, for instance, express amusement at how their partner suddenly started complimenting them for the first time in weeks after they happened to chat with an attractive man or woman at a social event. Others play on their partner's fears and anxieties; they engage in little acts to evoke jealousy, such as making eyes at a passing stranger and commenting on a "great bod."

The risk is that jealousy can easily move on its continuum from triggering mild anxiety (that can be exciting or enjoyable) to extreme anger and fear. Jealousy at the extreme can debilitate and destroy the relationship.

Perhaps jealousy is like a spice. With no spice, you can find the relationship dull and lacking in commitment. Add a little spice, and that keeps things interesting. But add too much spice, like when the lid pops off and the pepper pours in, and you can no longer enjoy the dish. The taste is much too strong.

Experiencing minor jealousy from time to time is usually not something to worry about. Especially is this true when you realize your fears aren't based in reality and the feeling doesn't linger. Your partner, for example, may have had an animated conversation with a person at a party, enjoyed it, and wants to share it with you. There's nothing to fear—in fact, the experience may make your relationship more vital.

Thus, it's best to just let go of everyday jealousies. Notice them, but don't dwell on them unless you have other trust issues. One of the worst solutions is to become possessive, demanding, or controlling. That will generally lead your partner to become defensive and result in the very loss of love you fear.

The Ways We Experience Jealousy

Besides being a continuum in intensity, jealousy reflects a mix of emotions that differs among people. It's as if each of us has our own jealousy genes, despite the fact that we may express jealousy in ways similar to others. That's because the internal triggers of jealousy are unique for each person.

Underlying triggers include feelings of fear, anger, pride, lust, joy, greed, and other emotions. For instance, one person may be driven by fear of losing a beloved and a sense of worth, while another person may be more influenced by a desire to maintain control and feelings of lust. As R. L. Barker writes in *The Green-Eyed Marriage*, "The numbers of different feeling components may be in the hundreds, but they add up to the totality we call jealousy. And the ingredients that constitute each person's unique jealousy keep changing with experiences, values, and circumstances of that person's life."

By identifying the situations that trigger jealous feelings and the intensity of those feelings, you are in a better position to control them. In addition, you can assess whether or not you are responding in a healthy way to a real warning sign, or if it is your fear leading you to overreact.

What's Real and What's Not

Whenever you experience pangs of jealousy, be it a minor concern or a deeper heartfelt one, you are responding to a perceived threat to your love relationship. Many types of situation can trigger this sense of danger. Whatever the trigger, the fear is that your lover might be taken from you, and underlying this fear is self-doubt. "Is there anything I have done wrong, anything to undermine my partner's love and affection?" Such doubts can spiral if you don't test your fears against the current reality.

In contrast, if you feel confident in yourself and in your partner's love and attraction, jealousy is experienced as less of an issue. It becomes a passing awareness.

Feeling threatened may also be left over from past experiences, leading you to perceive danger when there is none. For example, if your past suspicions had turned out to be justified, they may return to haunt you, even if there is no current basis in fact. One woman described walking hand in hand with her partner, feeling very close, when suddenly she was overcome by a strange suspicion. Her partner hadn't done anything to cause it, and soon she realized that some years before in that same area, she had spotted her steady beau with another woman, shattering her relationship.

Sometimes "the past" may go back to childhood. For example, if your father left the household when you were young, you may fear your husband is equally likely to abandon you. If one of your parents was alcoholic, workaholic, or depressed—unable to meet your needs—you may feel you don't deserve love; and if so, it is easy to feel threatened. And if as a child you were subject to strict discipline and discouraged from making your own decisions, you now may not feel in control of your life, and require lots of reassurance.

Unless you sort out the basis for suspicious feelings, the vague underlying force may remain disruptive. Since recurrent and intense jealousy can undermine any relationship, it is important to pay attention to what has led to suspicions in order to assess whether they are realistic rather than bubbling up from the past.

On the other hand, there are times when you might use your jealousy as a caution light to pay more attention to the relationship. In this case, avoid anything to make your partner feel defensive or to suggest you are being possessive. That would only compound any problems in your relationship. Rather, find positive ways to support the relationship and reinforce your feelings of mutual love and attraction.

Developing Positive Reactions to Jealousy

Because we differ in what makes each of us jealous and how intensely we feel it, we may respond in different ways, too. Sometimes, you may not even be aware that your behavior is triggered by jealousy; you may think something else is bothering you. If your partner is especially busy at work, for example, you may feel down in the dumps, bored, or lonely. In fact, you may be experiencing pangs of jealousy as well. Your feelings could easily rise to become full-fledged jealousy if another ingredient is added to the mix, such as when that work project lasts late into the night with someone whom your mate might find attractive.

Mild expressions of concern include the following:

- You pout or otherwise show your displeasure when your partner shows attention to someone else.
- You talk about the other person (whom your partner seems drawn to) in a disparaging way, highlighting what he or she has done wrong.
- You fish for compliments from your partner.
- You repeatedly ask your partner questions to gain reassurance of his or her love.
- You start watching your partner more closely for signs he or she is straying.

If you begin to behave in a jealous way, try to identify the feeling and understand the basis for your reaction. You are then in a better position to cope in a more positive manner, whether to protect yourself from a real threat, or to start ridding yourself of feelings that are unfounded.

In the initial, mild stages of jealousy, the concerns you express may be flattering to your partner. However, while at first they may have a positive effect, your jealousy is quite likely to have negative repercussions as you repeat them. Your partner may get defensive or retreat. And for you the danger is that repetition becomes draining emotionally, or your reactions may intensify. For example, instead of asking questions about what your partner has been doing in an easygoing, interested way, you may start making loud and angry accusations based on what you believe to be true. Even worse, you might threaten or confront the person you believe, correctly or incorrectly, is your rival.

Yet another danger sign is when your efforts to be watchful turn into attempts to secretly uncover evidence that your partner is lying to you or being unfaithful. Sometimes fear also leads to verbal or physical control in an effort to intimidate your partner. This is when jealousy is endangering your relationship. Put on the brakes.

While such extreme reactions are not common, it is not unheard of for loving relationships to turn into a nightmare of suspicions and recriminations, such as in the film *Fatal Attraction*. A woman (Glenn Close) couldn't bear to see the person with whom she was having an affair (Michael Douglas) pulling away from her. She began more and more intensely to attack her rival, her lover, and finally herself.

In contrast, you can respond to jealousy in more positive and productive ways. They increase your odds of overcoming any threats to your relationship.

Especially if your concern is serious, it is important to distinguish fact from fear. Ask yourself, "How much do I know, as opposed to how much I suspect without basis?" If you have solid proof that your partner is violating the faith of the relationship, it is time for a discussion. Have the discussion at a time when you are relatively calm. Avoid accusing, condemning or otherwise passing judgment on your partner. Talk about *your* feelings of concern and vulnerability, not the shortcomings of your partner.

Even after a productive discussion, you may not be able to erase your suspicions, but you can make an effort to stop them from dominating your life. One simple but effective technique is called *thought-stopping*. As soon as you begin to think of your partner with someone else, for instance, break your concentration by saying out loud or to yourself, "Stop! Here I go again, dragging myself down. Let it go." Then focus your attention outward, attend to something upbeat, breathe deeply, send the message to your muscles to loosen and relax. You may not be able to force your mind to stop thinking disturbing thoughts but you can gently distract yourself.

For mild feelings of jealousy where the threat is small, it is not a bad idea to use the opportunity to improve yourself:

- Dress more attractively to attract your partner's favorable attention once again. Sometimes in a long-term relationship, we can take our partner for granted and let the way we dress slip. But if you can imagine how you dressed for your partner when you were dating and courting, this can add a new excitement to your relationship. It is a small yet productive step toward renewal.

- Develop your skills or abilities so you outshine any potential rival. For example, if your partner is looking outside the relationship for more stimulating conversation, do some extra reading, take a class, or find a new hobby you enjoy. This way you'll not only experience personal growth, but your partner may appreciate you more.
- Engage in something new just because your partner finds it worthwhile. Take notice of your partner's activities, not in an effort to pry and uncover evidence but to gain more insight into what your partner likes to do; learn more about it in order to participate in that activity with your partner.

Most important of all, do not allow your partner's interest in someone or something else to result in a loss of your personal worth. That is a serious and emotionally costly mistake. You have the responsibility to maintain your own sense of worth regardless of someone else's judgment or actions. Any time you give your sense of well-being over to another person's care you are putting yourself in jeopardy, regardless of who the person is. Talk to yourself and challenge your thinking on this matter; ask yourself, "Why have you suddenly become less of a person simply because your partner is neglecting the relationship?"

In short, jealousy is a defense to a perceived threat. If you use that mechanism in a positive way, you can clarify whether the danger is real. If so, you can respond to it in a manner that may strengthen rather than undermine your relationship.

Overcoming Feelings of Inadequacy

As we've seen, sometimes jealousy springs not so much from a situation as from deep-seated uncertainties about your self-worth, or from an inability to trust yourself. With that type of predisposition, you are likely to read almost anything your partner does as a sign of rejection, loss of interest, or a drifting away from you. You may even imagine putdowns and acts to harm you where none are meant.

A classic Alfred Hitchcock thriller, *Suspicion*, reflects the way a poor self-image can lead to intense jealous suspicion. In the film, the heroine imagines that her charming, flirtatious husband is doing everything to take advantage of her, even do her in. She sees everything he does through a lens of suspicion until his true virtue is revealed in the end.

Intense and continuing or recurring jealousy is a signal to look within, since people who feel emotionally secure, self-confident, and accepting of themselves rarely have such deeply jealous feelings. A number of research studies by social scientists (described in *The Green-Eyed Marriage*) have found that people with serious jealousy problems are more likely to have been troubled by inferiority and inadequacy. Thus the thought of losing someone to another person becomes so devastating; you fear that the other person is more worthy and, consequently, wouldn't want to be with you. The accompanying desperation tempts you to use intimidation or manipulation to hold onto the other person. Such efforts often result in further alienating the loved one. Ironically, the jealous lover then confirms a lack of worth and feels even more inadequate.

Some psychologists believe that intense jealous feelings reflect not so much love but dependency. It's the kind of love psychologist Abraham Maslow has described in *Toward a Psychology of Being* as "D-love," deficiency-based love. (In contrast, "B-love," being in love, is a mature circumstance in which both partners are fully committed to each other's well-being and happiness.) The problem with "D-love," which is often at the root of intense jealousy, is that it is selfish and needy, derived from feelings of inadequacy. The other person's love, constant attention, and presence feels as vital for survival as oxygen.

Thus, if you do have intensely jealous feelings that might be triggered by strong self-doubts and a powerful feeling of neediness, you need to address these underlying concerns. You need to take steps to build up your own feelings of self-worth, so you can believe in and trust yourself again.

Professional help may be in order, although there are some things you can do on your own, at least to begin. Among them:

- Think of all the things you do well. Make a list of your various skills and abilities. Write down all the things people have

complimented you about. Make a note of all your good qualities. Then, review this list and repeat it to yourself again and
again. You can even paste notes with these statements on a
wall or the refrigerator. Use affirmations to remind yourself of
your many positive qualities.

- Join a support group for people who are struggling with jealousy problems or have joined together in an effort to improve
their self-esteem. If you are unable to locate the right group,
start your own.

- Spend one day paying close attention to your self-talk, those
inner conversations you are always having with yourself. What
do you notice? If you find that you are hard on yourself,
putting yourself down for mistakes, perfectionistic in your
standards, consider this: All of us are fallible; even those you
most admire are flawed. If you take the position that you have
to improve in order to be worthy, you'll never embrace yourself.
The only way to increase your self-esteem is to accept yourself—problems, limitations, and flaws all included. Those of us
who are withholding the embrace until we are worthy have a
long wait. Each of us is a work in progress that will be left
unfinished at the end our life.

When intense jealousy is triggered by internal self-doubt, self-exam-
ination can help you conquer your feelings of jealousy as well as problems in your relationship caused by your jealous responses. Certainly,
feel free to make yourself more appealing to your mate, such as dressing more attractively and developing your skills and abilities. But work
on building yourself up internally as well, because that is where the real
issue lies.

Rating Your Experience of Jealousy

Your experience of jealousy actually breaks down into three major
pieces: physical responses, emotional responses, and thoughts. Negative
thoughts trigger your mix of physical and emotional responses, so if you
work on changing your thoughts to those that are self-affirming and
accepting, you can transform your negative physical actions and emotional disturbance as well.

Then, too, you can also work on changing your behaviors or redirecting your negative emotions, so you feel better and behave more productively when you feel jealous. For example, if being jealous makes you nervous and shaky, consciously choose to do something else you enjoy that distracts you. If you tend to react with rage and aggression, redirect this energy into athletic activity.

A jealousy assessment can be a first step to better understanding how you respond, enabling you to quickly identify and work on physical, emotional, or thought responses—on your own, in a support group, or with a therapist.

RECOGNIZING HOW YOU RESPOND TO FEELINGS OF JEALOUSY

How Intense Are Your Responses? (Circle your usual response.)

	HIGH	MEDIUM	LOW	NONE
Physical Reactions				
Feel nervous/shaky	3	2	1	0
Feel faint	3	2	1	0
Feel my head pounding	3	2	1	0
Feel my heart pounding	3	2	1	0
Lose my appetite	3	2	1	0
Can't sleep well	3	2	1	0
Other: (indicate)				
_____	3	2	1	0
_____	3	2	1	0
Emotional Responses				
Feel very sad	3	2	1	0
Feel helpless	3	2	1	0
Feel fearful	3	2	1	0
Feel anger	3	2	1	0
Feel hostility/hatred	3	2	1	0
Feel put down/humiliated	3	2	1	0
Feel envious	3	2	1	0
Other: (indicate)				
_____	3	2	1	0
_____	3	2	1	0

	HIGH	MEDIUM	LOW	NONE
What I Think				
I blame myself	3	2	1	0
I pity myself	3	2	1	0
I think I'm not good enough	3	2	1	0
I think about my loss	3	2	1	0
I think I've been bested	3	2	1	0
I think I've been left out	3	2	1	0
I imagine getting revenge	3	2	1	0
I resent my rival	3	2	1	0
Other: (indicate)				
_____	3	2	1	0
_____	3	2	1	0

Assessing What Makes You Jealous

To better understand what makes you jealous—and whether your perception of the situation is realistic—examine how you respond to situations that evoke jealous feelings in many people. Here is an assessment tool. You can use it with your mate as well to better understand each other and discuss when these issues interfere with your trust. This will also help you set ground rules for acceptable behavior and for boundaries during those situations. (If the situations that make you or your partner jealous aren't listed, add your own.)

THE SITUATIONS THAT MAKE YOU JEALOUS

A Starting Point for Discussion

How Jealous Do You Feel? (Circle your usual response.)

	HIGH	MEDIUM	LOW	NONE
At a Social Gathering				
My partner flirts and dances closely with others	3	2	1	0
My partner spends a great deal of time talking to someone else	3	2	1	0

	HIGH	MEDIUM	LOW	NONE
My partner disappears for a long time at a party	3	2	1	0
Other:_____	3	2	1	0

On the Phone

	HIGH	MEDIUM	LOW	NONE
I call my partner and keep getting a busy signal	3	2	1	0
When I get through my partner has little time for me	3	2	1	0

With Others

	HIGH	MEDIUM	LOW	NONE
My partner has a lover	3	2	1	0
My partner has a good friend who could be sexually attractive to my partner	3	2	1	0
My partner has a number of single friends	3	2	1	0
My partner says positive things about an acquaintance or an associate at work	3	2	1	0
My partner makes complimentary remarks about strangers	3	2	1	0
My partner says positive things about a celebrity or film star	3	2	1	0
Other:_____	3	2	1	0

Interpreting Your Responses

This assessment lists items in order of what most commonly evokes jealousy. The last items are generally *not* provocative.

If you feel jealous when your partner is clearly involved with someone else, that's understandable. However, if you become easily jealous—if you are provoked by situations that lack real intrusion, this signals you may be overly jealous and may have problems with self-regard and self-trust.

On the other hand, if you don't respond with any jealous feelings, this suggests that you don't value the relationship very much, are unusually nonjealous, or perhaps have an uncommonly "open" relationship with your partner. (Frankly, such relationships are often hard to maintain free of jealousy.)

The Dynamics of Jealousy in a Relationship

In deciding how to best handle a jealousy flare-up, consider not only *your* feelings and reactions, but your partner's—and the interplay between them. Are there patterns or cycles of jealousy in your relationship? It is not uncommon for couples to use jealousy as camouflage to conceal other problems.

Typically, we choose our mates to fulfill a particular role; and our relationship is based, in part, on complementary personality traits. For example, a logical, cognitively oriented person may choose a love partner who is more emotional. The emotion-based person, in effect, carries the feelings for the couple. In addition, as we've seen, we are all influenced by childhood experiences and project those memories and associations onto a love interest.

Psychological dynamics and projections may show up as interpersonal games, including games based on issues of jealousy and mistrust. Noted psychiatrist Eric Berne popularized a series of these games, such as *Uproar; See What You Made Me Do; If It Weren't For You;* and *Yes, But . . .* that can be played out with a jealousy theme. If you look closely at jealousy outbreaks that repeat, you may find patterns that will help you better understand what's going on and offer clues on how to deal with this issue.

For example, in one troubled marriage, Jerry kept accusing Amanda of being unfaithful with no basis in reality. Jerry would notice her spending a long time on the phone and question her closely about whom she just spoke to. Was it really her girlfriend—or a secret lover? He would also confront her about whether supermarket trips were a chance for secret trysts, or whether a glance at an attractive passing man might mean she was thinking about making love to him.

At base, Jerry's concerns reflected his own suppressed impulses to be unfaithful, which he projected onto his wife. By noticing when Amanda might be straying, and by exaggerating the import of her activities, he was able to keep his own unconscious impulses in check.

In another example, George was deeply jealous of his wife Betty; his childhood experiences had led him to deeply mistrust any woman. He had seen his mother, an alcoholic, participating in a number of affairs when his father was away, and he knew to stay away from the house when one of his mother's lovers was there. He could tell by seeing another car parked in front of the house or in the driveway, so he would wait outside, fuming angrily about what his mother was doing, though unable to express his anger. When his father discovered one of the affairs, threatened to kill his mother, and had a heart attack, resulting in his hospitalization for several weeks, George's anger worsened.

It is no wonder George had a difficult time trusting women and had a strong need to feel in control. His first marriage was to a woman he didn't love as a way of avoiding his intense feelings of jealousy. He picked a woman who was mousy, shy, and not particularly attractive. Eventually, he drifted away from her out of boredom and they divorced.

Shortly afterward, he met Betty, a very attractive woman who excited him. She was like an overcorrection for his first wife. Betty had learned much from being with other men and fulfilled him as never before. What's more, Betty was determined to put aside her promiscuous past.

After they married, Betty was true to her commitment to strict monogamy. Yet George's jealousy would break out at odd times, typically while they were making love. Suddenly, he would stop caressing her and push her away, as if he couldn't touch her. He was imagining his wife having sex with the other men in her past. He was sure she was negatively comparing him to them, although she would reassure him that her lovemaking with him was special because she so deeply loved him; it wasn't like the casual sex of her past.

In time it became apparent George was projecting onto Betty his internalized image of his unfaithful mother and his rage about her affairs. He was also projecting his own wish to be like his "immoral, lascivious, unfaithful" mother. A forbidden part of him, kept secret even from himself, desired to act out sexually. It wanted to do what he was falsely accusing Betty of doing. His impulses were activated during lovemaking; then his moral censor would come into play, causing him to turn off and push Betty away.

Fortunately, George was receptive to couple therapy, and he and Betty were able to understand the dynamics that led to his unreasonable jealousy. Once the underlying dynamics were exposed, George could counter his game of *Jealous Uproar* and the relationship began to heal.

Playing Jealousy Games

Sometimes, patterns of jealousy get established because of the reward or payoff for engaging in jealous behavior. A cycle of jealousy, accusation, and denial, often followed by making up, apologies, exciting lovemaking, avowals of love, and other behaviors to reaffirm the relationship, is rewarding. The process is also like a game, *Let's Fight and Then Make Love*; it could have dangerous results if you play too hard or lose control. It's like climbing a mountain for fun, going too high, and then being unable to descend.

Fun—At First

Consider John and Patricia's marriage, which nearly foundered due to John's growing jealousy. Initially, Patricia enjoyed teasing John about the appeal of the men she flirted with; she even kidded him about how attractive she found the male newscaster on a news program she liked to watch. She found it exciting to see John get riled up and become more attentive because of the mild threat of losing her affection to someone else.

Before long, however, it became apparent that John's jealousy was getting out of hand. He began accusing her of flirting, yelling at her if she seemed more attentive than usual when she watched the news, and admonishing her for "dressing like a tramp" to attract men. Clearly, what began as fun, a teasing game that added excitement to the relationship, turned into a serious rift between them that threatened their marriage.

It became so destructive because it brought up troubling issues from John's childhood. While Patricia had come from a warm, loving home, John came from a family in which his parents were often distant and he spent many hours in his room alone, feeling ignored. Patricia's teasing triggered John's insecurities, and led him to either snarl at her in anger or retreat into a sullen shell as he did as a child.

Not the Real Issue

Another way that playing a jealousy game can be rewarding yet destructive, is when it satisfies some unconscious wish or motive. The process can continue for some time without escalating into the danger zone; but by playing the game, a couple may keep themselves from resolving important issues. In some instances, for example, a couple may engage in jealous behavior because it defends them against other more painful or serious emotional upsets. They might find the fighting resulting from jealous feelings a welcome release for emotions they can't otherwise express, as in *Who's Afraid of Virginia Woolf,* where a couple fights continuously to avoid facing the pain of blame for a child who died. Another basis for triggering a jealous or angry response is to give one a sense of power and control over the other partner.

In an almost endless variety of maneuvers, jealous behavior can mask something beneath the surface. Sometimes a person who is otherwise emotionally constricted uses jealousy to express his or her feelings. For example, a man might suddenly start yelling at his partner for some real or imagined offense that suggests unfaithfulness. Despite denials, he continues the barrage, until his emotions are released in a kind of catharsis. A person may even set up the suspicious situation such as by bringing a colleague home for dinner, then leaving to run a quick errand. Accusations of being disloyal "behind my back" later trigger an argument, releasing emotions that may or may not have some basis in the relationship.

This cycle can be triggered by a partner who feels inadequate and is using jealousy to avoid intimacy or sex. For example, Danny's feelings of inadequacy often left him unable to respond sexually. Rather than be embarrassed about poor performance in the bedroom, he triggered a jealousy outburst, sidetracking any sexual contact. He felt more comfortable spending the night on the couch than possibly failing in bed.

It may come down to this: Partners who are chronically angry and fighting over jealousy are probably banging away at the wrong issues. What if jealousy were not the issue? Would something else surface? Honest self-scrutiny is required. Consider only that your own feelings may need work, for you cannot control your partner.

Research reported in *Romantic Jealousy* by Ayala Pines suggests that people who report a high degree of jealousy share several traits. They have a low opinion of themselves, a large gap between how they are and how they would like to be, and value highly such visible achievements as becoming wealthy, famous, well-liked and, especially, physically attractive. Jealousy is most likely to be provoked in the area of a person's greatest desires—a person who longs to be rich is most vulnerable if a lover shows attention to someone wealthy, for example. Therefore it is wise to be on the alert for your Achilles' heel. This is an instance in which responding with your head rather than your heart is prudent.

Fair fighting, that is, fighting in which both partners are striving to resolve a conflict rather than destroy an opponent, is also required. A couple can tell if it fights poorly by the results—one or both partners are constantly hurt and conflicts are hardly ever resolved.

Even under the best of circumstances, manipulative emotional games will be played occasionally, but as side events, not center-stage attractions. As partners are able to trust that it is safe to express one's true feelings, games of manipulation will yield to healthy and open communication. If this is not occurring and the fighting is unproductive, it is time to seek professional assistance.

THE FRONTIER OF TRUST

SEXUAL FIDELITY

Accidental Detection?

I was going to a psychologist at the time and I remember telling him I thought my husband was seeing other women. He kept asking why I was so untrusting and insecure. He confused me and my husband confused me.

Yet I was right after all. My instincts weren't wrong. I found out through my husband's diary that he was having affairs. He was also seen with her at a restaurant we frequently ate at. I was appalled. I begged him to stop. I carried on. I screamed, "If you loved me, you wouldn't do this!" I ranted and raved and thought I was going to have a nervous breakdown.

It took a long time for me to calm down that evening. I felt like killing him, and at one point I even got up to get a kitchen knife. I was frightened; frightened I might turn it on myself.

During the course of the night, he made a clean breast of a whole lot of things he'd been doing over the past years; different women, women in his office, old friends of ours, business arrangements, and that sort of thing. He said none of it had been important to him; not one person. And he swore he'd change, give it all up. I believed him; it sounded as if he was honest. I assumed my crying and misery had had an impact on him.

He was very apologetic, and during the next year he kept bringing home gifts for me. He was generally more thoughtful than he'd ever been. I was flattered, reassured, and I began to trust him again.

Then there was this night when we were driving by his office after a movie, and he suggested we go up and screw on the rug. I found that very romantic. It was a Saturday night, the building was dark and empty; I felt as if this was a clandestine kind of thing and was very excited. I really got into a whole fantasy about it. After we made love and had gotten dressed, he went into the bathroom.

He was taking a really long time, and I was sitting behind his desk waiting for him. After a while, I opened a drawer and staring me in the face was a letter that started out, "To my lover." Just then I heard him come out of the bathroom, and I grabbed the letter and put it in my pocket. When he came over to embrace me, I maneuvered around him saying I had to go now: "It must have been something we ate." In the bathroom, I read the letter. I was shocked.

The letter was from a woman he worked with. It was a love letter. She described her feelings about an evening they had spent together the previous week. I remember that night. I wanted his companionship; I felt lonely. He told me he had a dinner date with a potentially important customer from out of town. "It's one of those things," he had said. The bastard!

The letter mentioned me. This woman said she was jealous of me; she couldn't stand separating from him. She wanted him all for herself. She described some very private moments they shared.

I felt as if someone had cut me open and pulled out my insides. Never have I felt so exposed, so vulnerable, betrayed. I trusted him; he had promised to stop a year ago when I was so distressed, but even then he wasn't honest. I threw up. After a while, I came out of the bathroom, and although I was shivering all night as if I were in shock, I didn't let on I knew anything. I was too frightened of the implications to do anything.

When one partner discovers that the other is having an affair, the reaction is often profound shock followed by hurt, anger, and a complete shattering of trust. The woman describing her experience above detected infidelity twice. A diary left open, a letter not destroyed, an indiscreet choice of meeting places—did these have a deliberate element? Sexual betrayal itself was bad enough—a nuclear assault on trust, but did this most serious breach convey a message with an unconscious intent?

Obviously, keeping sexual activities a total secret from one's partner takes some work. Besides being caught in the act, the most dramatic disclosure of all, the risks are innumerable: an automobile accident; an injury to a child that causes a frightened parent to contact a mate who is not at the stated place; a chance encounter with a relative; an unpredicted change in plans by a mate; a suspicious pregnancy; and sexually transmitted diseases, which can be tough to explain if one's mate is afflicted.

This is to say nothing of changes in attitude and behavior at home that arouse a mate's suspicions. In addition, there are telltale signs of clandestine sexual enthusiasm—smudged lipstick, perfume traces, bites, bruises, and scratches garnered in the heat of passion.

Mental health practitioners are familiar with the man or woman who is so careless with incriminating evidence that "accidental" detection is a sure thing. Sometimes the evidence is unconsciously left by a lover to make trouble at home and force a separation. Or it may be a way of forcing the hand of a mate who refuses to acknowledge that the relationship is in trouble.

Neither is it unknown for the involved partner to summon attention by flaunting the affair. Detection may also serve the purpose of partners who want their mates to dissolve the relationship. Of course, most people do not willingly acknowledge that their brazenness conveys such purposes.

Nor is the intended effect usually achieved. A man who is indiscreetly conducting an affair may wish to force his partner to pay more attention to him; but the partner may have been disgusted with the relationship for some time, and this brazenness at last provides a pretext for breakup. Or a woman who is trying to provoke her partner into walking out on her may find herself trapped when her partner uses the detected affair as emotional and financial blackmail, threatening to leave her with nothing and to reveal her to the children and her parents.

Occasionally, a person will deny a mate's obvious affair involvement because acknowledgment may be so threatening to his or her sense of trust and security that it cannot be tolerated.

Arthur, a large man with imposing stature, was a biologist in his early forties who specialized in cancer research. He was not the type of man easily forgotten. His direct, assertive manner left an impression on most people—they either appreciated him dearly or felt threatened and intimidated. His wife Beth also made a notable impression. Though not as gregarious as her husband, she makes up for it with her striking looks and quiet, keen intellect.

The couple sought professional help for "communication difficulties." Frequently, this catchall statement masks more specific dissatisfactions. It turned out that Arthur wanted his wife to be more affectionate and sexual with him. Beth wanted him to stop making so much of an issue about sex: "You know I am not a naturally affectionate person!" Arthur complained that his wife spent too much time away from home, and worse yet, as soon as she came in from an evening's volunteer work, would announce she had a headache, felt fatigued, or give some other excuse that would preclude sexual intimacy.

Complaints, countercomplaints, and dissatisfaction were longstanding in the marriage. For a year Arthur had been feeling particularly sexually deprived and resentful. However, he never dared raise any question as to his wife's sexual trustworthiness. Halfway into their first therapy session together, the following dialogue took place:

BETH: *And another thing, you seem to resent my going out at night. The charity organizations I work for depend on me and that's important to me. All you worry about is how you can get in touch with me. I keep telling you I don't know which part of the hospital will be available for our meetings.*

THERAPIST: *Beth, you seem to be implying that your husband doesn't trust you. Is that so?*

BETH: (beginning to blush) *Yes, either that or he is trying to control me and resents my independence.*

THERAPIST: *In what way might he not trust you?*

BETH: (neck and face crimson red) *I don't know; you'll have to ask him.*

ARTHUR: (sitting stiffly and staring away from his wife's obvious emotional reaction to the therapist's probe) *I'm not trying to control my wife; I would just like to see more of her.*

At this point, the therapist did not pursue the possibility of affair involvement any further and at the end of the hour arranged to see Beth the following week without her husband. Assured of confidentiality, she acknowledged an affair that had been going on for a little over a year.

Arthur, a bright, scientifically trained, socially aware man, had come face-to-face with his wife's adultery, but he had blinded himself to the evidence. Probably a fair number of men and women employ the same defense of denial. To confront the breach of trust that sexual infidelity represents takes a great degree of courage—courage to face the pain that lies ahead.

True Confessions

In contrast to the affair that is practically flaunted only to be ignored, in some instances a suspicious lover will hire a detective to gather clear evidence. This tactic is usually employed at the urging of a lawyer, and even then with reluctance because it is humiliating to both partners.

More commonly, some people feel impelled to confess their sexual adventures to their mate. The motives behind voluntary confessions vary; guilt and the need to be forgiven, along with a hope for renewed trust, are probably the most common. Typically the one who confessed becomes the target of anger, hostility, or shame. After punishment, that person may hope to feel cleansed and restored to innocence. But that result is rare, as Paul's story attests:

I had this nagging guilt. My wife and I are close; we share things together and have a commitment to each other. My deception about the affair really bothered me. There were a number of underhanded things I noticed myself doing to ease my discomfort. For example, I would come home and be very critical, provoke fights, in fact. What I really wanted was for Joyce to say, "You son of a bitch, go to hell!" Something that would relieve me of my responsibility. This way I could say to myself, "Well, we're on the outs; the old rules are null and void."

The problem is that Joyce is so tolerant of me that it didn't work. I couldn't get her to give up on me. I also tried flirting in front of her, hoping that she would take the hint and give me permission, like, "Okay, I can see you want to make it with another woman, go ahead, be my guest." That didn't work either, she wasn't about to offer her best wishes—that tolerant she wasn't. After a while, being too damned honest and conscientious for my own good, I couldn't keep things secret from her.

It happened like this: We were at a party and Susan Fields was there. I said to my wife, "I want to leave; let's get out of here! There is something I have to talk to you about." She said, "What's wrong?" and I told her that we'd discuss it on the way home. As we drove away from the party, I told her about my affair with Susan.

It was a mistake; I knew it as soon as I started because her face flushed in a real scary sort of way, but it was too late. Her voice cracked as she asked me a lot of questions. Then she sort of curled up within herself and suffered in silence.

If she had fought me, it might have turned me against her, and I could deal with that. But she was so hurt and so deeply unhappy, I couldn't handle it. Neither could she. We survived, but it left quite a scar on both of us.

When suspicion and mistrust arising out of unfaithfulness are blocking intimacy and the deceived partner keeps probing the issue, a frank discussion, preferably with the help of a therapist, may improve the relationship. Of course, even at this juncture some people may choose not to be candid. A person remaining with a partner for expediency's sake—for instance, a wife with several children who has no hope of employment, and who wants nothing from the marriage except financial support—may continue to lie in an effort to maintain the relationship. But those who wish to improve things and foster mutual trust would best consider honesty.

In cases such as Paul's where one's mate suspects little or nothing, "enlightenment" seldom serves a constructive purpose and may well severely disturb the unsuspecting. The confessor not only doesn't return to innocence, but frequently feels even more like a heel. Both parties are now in acute distress and the issue of damaged trust is likely to haunt them for a long while.

This is a large price to pay when the need to confess is not much more than a self-serving act to relieve guilt cloaked in a wish to renegotiate the relationship. The lack of wisdom in this type of behavior was confirmed by leading professionals specializing in love relations, in a 1970 symposium in the journal *Medical Aspects of Human Sexuality:*

- Carlton B. Broderick, director of marriage and family counselor training at the University of Southern California, wrote:

  Like any other remedy, confession of extramarital affairs to a spouse is only helpful under certain conditions. I have cases where such a confession set marital therapy back several weeks and at least two instances where it disrupted the marriage completely. Indeed, the potential for damage is so real that I have become a conservative on this issue.

- Harold Winn, clinical professor of psychiatry at Temple University Medical Center, asked: "Should a husband or wife confess infidelity?" and answered: "In general, the response to this question is No." He pointed out that abrupt confessions may relieve the guilt of the adulterer, but frequently will not be taken well by the other partner, and may actually be an act of conscious or unconscious hostility.

- Charles E. Llewellyn, professor of psychiatry at Duke University Medical Center, added his view:

  Should a husband or wife confess infidelity? An informal poll of friends, secretaries, colleagues, and students yielded a unanimous "No," but many elaborated their answers in some form. . . . In my opinion a husband or wife should not confess infidelity to the other unless he or she feels it necessary. I recommend that the

> *involved partner discuss the situation with someone who is quali-*
> *fied to understand and work with the complexities of the situa-*
> *tion and its meaning to the potential confessor, to the spouse, and*
> *to the marriage.*

- A high-ranking clergyman, Bishop James Pike, wrote that when two lovers have decided an affair is justifiable, they may have an obligation to lie about it for the good of the others: "Once a primary ethical decision has been made a particular way, more often than not secondary ethical responsibilities (i.e., secrecy and deception) are entailed."

Is all this to say that honesty and trustworthiness between love part-ners had best be thrown to the wind? No. The point is simply that most of us, in response to, "Did you have a nice day, dear?" are not ready for, "Oh yes, I spent the morning at a business meeting and spent the after-noon with a terrific lover, screwing to my heart's content. And how was your day, dear?" When a mate is unsuspecting, then what's suggested is discretion, consideration, tact, and courteous selectivity.

That's one of the limitations of an affair: the joy of it does not lend itself to sharing with one's partner. When the issue is illicit sex, a "true confession" in the spirit of full disclosure is especially likely to produce panic and pain, rather than permanence and peace.

Panic and Pain

The desire to be special to someone, to be "number one," to be wanted above all others, probably burns in all of us. No matter that this is an unrealistic ideal; the ground rules of traditional relationships attempt to secure it via sexual exclusivity. To most of us, a clandestine affair con-stitutes a breach of trust, a violation of the implicitly agreed-upon rules. When the deception is discovered, emotions ranging from panic to furious rage are common. Behavior varies from immobility to violence.

Some people may be so secure that they are not much threatened by the discovery of their partner's affair; they respond with tolerance, understanding, and calm. But they are as rare as living saints. Even those who have been having secret liaisons of their own react with deep shock, anger, and jealousy when they discover that their partner has been doing the same!

Some people, so hurt by the experience, will view infidelity as unforgivable and will move to break up the relationship. Others will see it as a symptom of what has been lacking in their relationship and will set out to do something about it. Still others will view it as not symptomatic of anything in particular and work toward a mutual agreement about such behavior. And there are those who will "stick it out" for reasons of economics, insecurity, or children, but will have only a cold, trustless relationship.

Sometimes the discovery of an affair merely heightens a conflict that has been developing because of the emotion and time being drawn from the relationship. This is most likely to occur when the affair is time-consuming and emotionally absorbing. Of course, it is possible that more, rather than less, emotion will flow into the relationship as a result of an affair. Unfortunately, the effect is most often one of conflict, suspicion, and intense insecurity.

When two persons have gotten along together reasonably well and trust conflicts have not been prominent, one episode of infidelity will rarely trigger a separation. It may produce shock and resentment, and sometimes even physical estrangement, but not a sudden ending. When an affair ends the relationship, it is usually the last straw after a slow, prolonged deterioration of trust.

Where the affair involvement is casual, the effect on the relationship may be very small until the affair is discovered. Then it is primarily the knowledge of the affair rather than the affair per se that is disruptive and trust-damaging.

Coping with Broken Trust: Destructive Tactics

The effect of a discovered affair on the trust in a relationship depends also on other factors. What motivated the affair, was it driven mainly by "want" or by "need"? Even more critical is the other partner's interpretation of what the affair means. Consider this example:

> My mate, who is having an affair, does not love me anymore and cannot bear to have me around because I am stupid, boring, annoying,

insensitive, and incompetent. Furthermore, I am sexually inadequate. This breach is going to finish us. What will others think if they find out about our problems?

Obviously, partners who think like that will feel and act differently from those who do not conclude from the experience that they are inadequate and their relationship is hopeless.

Most of us have inflated sex to unrealistic proportions. For one thing, we equate it with intimacy. This is true sometimes, but certainly not always; sex is frequently not intimate, and intimacy often does not include sex.

Moreover, infidelity, loosely defined as a breach of trust, occurs in many facets of a relationship—why is it that the sexual aspect usually brings on the strongest reaction? This leads to some disproportionate reactions. People may be destroyed by their partner's affair, even if assured it is casual and nonintimate, but fairly unconcerned by a mate's involvement in an intimate nonsexual exchange that is guaranteed to stay nonsexual.

The point here is that illicit sex, like all behavior, is open to many interpretations; and the interpretation chosen shapes the feelings generated.

Guilt to the Hilt

One who becomes distraught upon learning of a mate's affair has several choices in expressing that feeling. One can, for example, proceed to suffer in grand and glorious style, all the while hoping that the mate will be moved by the pain and prove true love by rejecting the outside relationship:

MATE ONE: (letting her lip tremble just so) *If you don't stop running around, we might as well get a divorce.*

MATE TWO: (in frustrated anger) *Don't be silly. You don't really want a divorce!*

MATE ONE: *I do! Don't you care about our marriage and what I'll have to go through being single again?*

MATE TWO: (feeling guilty) *Of course I care! What kind of a person do you think I am? I do a lot of things for you!*

MATE ONE: *You're selfish. You only do things that you care about. If you really cared about our marriage, you wouldn't have anyone else on your mind. It's all your fault that I'm eating too much and getting fat. I do it out of the frustration you cause. You're going to drive me to suicide!*

This approach is characteristic of the wronged mate who is passive and timid. The hurt is turned inward and is expressed in the form of accident, neglect of health, suicide attempts, and other self-destructive, "victim" behaviors. In the type of communication just illustrated, emotional distress is used as a tool to manipulate the involved mate. The object here is not direct and honest expression of authentic feelings; it is to induce guilt in the involved partner and thereby control behavior. The message is: "Stop what you are doing or I shall be even more miserable." This attempt to control a partner through guilt is often accompanied by an appeal to duty: "You owe it to me to stop seeing her."

The pairing of a self-pitying moralist such as this and a guilt-prone adulterer sets up a destructive interaction. Moralists can play prosecutor, judge, and jury on one occasion, and then, in the second role as victim, feel assaulted, rejected, and sorry for themselves, all the while provoking a guilty squirm or a flurry of angry self-defense from the affair-involved partner.

But this ploy has its disadvantages. As Bertrand Russell has written, "In former days parents ruined their relations with children by preaching love as a duty; husbands and wives still too often ruin their relations to each other by the same mistake. Love cannot be a duty because it is not subject to the will."

Replaying the guilt/duty message often enough can exert a strong influence. Even if the unfaithful partner is a low-guilt type, it frequently plays upon a dislike of disruption at home and fear of being disgraced if the indiscretions become publicized. The impact is so potent that it sometimes terminates the relationship along with the affair:

My wife and I had what I could call a guarded relationship. There were several touchy areas that we both avoided. When she found out about my other involvement, she initially used an appeal to sympathy (tears, outcries, visible suffering); then she resorted to what she called a "reduction of services" (cold dinners, uncooperativeness, and the like); and then the final blow . . .

One night, I came home late from a business meeting (I had stopped seeing other women months before) and she was lying unconscious in the middle of the living-room floor. There was an empty bottle of sleeping pills nearby where I couldn't miss them. I called the police and we took her to the emergency room where her stomach was pumped. She stayed overnight at the hospital and was released the following afternoon.

That was it. The last straw. I couldn't take it anymore. I felt like a complete heel all over again. Suppose I hadn't come home when I did and she had succeeded? How could I live with that? How could I leave the house every day not knowing what she would do? I was frantic. How could I face anyone who found out what this was all about? For the first time in months, I started to consider leaving again. I just couldn't take the pressure anymore.

Trying Too Hard

Occasionally, a man or woman whose partner is unfaithful will make a desperate effort to "get his act together." A man may lose weight, become more discerning about his dress and general appearance, and be extremely attentive to his partner in an effort to compete with the third party. Following the suggestions of many women's magazines, a woman will make a concerted effort to be seductive, sexy, and passionate. But anger, hurt, and jealousy are hardly conducive to such behavior and frequently desperate measures backfire.

Dori and Alvin are in their early forties. Two weeks before, Dori discovered that Alvin was having an affair. Since then, he ended the affair and she has been trying to deny her distress. Her attempts to play up to Alvin are both an effort to keep him and a distraction from her emotional pain. They have just finished having intercourse. She has pretended passion, but she is not a good actress:

ALVIN: *You don't seem to be getting much out of this anymore.*

DORI: *Oh no, I enjoy it.*

ALVIN: *You don't seem to enjoy it like you used to.*

DORI: (her bitterness getting the best of her) *You're not like you used to be.*

ALVIN: (feeling angry) *What the hell does that mean?*

DORI: *Oh, Alvin, forget it. In a while, things will be better again. Let's give it some time.*

ALVIN: (his guilt and anger rising) *I suppose you're referring to that thing with Florence Jackson.*

DORI: *I don't want to talk about that!*

ALVIN: *Look, these things happen. Nobody's perfect!*

DORI: *All right, then, I'm not perfect either. Let's forget it.*

ALVIN: *Forget it, my ass. You won't let me forget, that's clear from the cold shoulder you've been giving me in bed.*

DORI: *I never turn you down.*

ALVIN: *But you never turn me on either. You go through the motions, but it's empty.*

DORI: *Alvin, don't push me. I'm doing all I can.*

ALVIN: (still feeling provoked and guilty) *Do you think I like making love to a woman who's cold? This must be your way of getting back!*

DORI: *I'm not getting back at you. I'm trying to forget it! It's just that I have trouble feeling the same way I used to. Maybe in time it will get better. Time heals all wounds.*

ALVIN: *If you want to call it quits, just let me know.*

DORI: (her suppressed anger surfacing) *So you can get back together with your girlfriend!*

ALVIN: *Oh, for cryin' out loud, I've told you . . .*

And so on. This kind of communication barely scratches the surface. If denial and avoidance were not so prominent, this couple might have taken the opportunity to examine the basic issues: their feelings and attitudes toward each other; the circumstances and causes of the affair; and whether it was a single, chance occurrence or reflects feelings that warrant ending the relationship.

Revenge Is Sour

Sometimes a hurt, distressed mate tries retaliation. For example, if John has an affair with Helen, a friend of his wife Mary, then Mary may begin to go to bed with all of John's friends, and after doing so, throw it in his face. The result of this contest to see who can hurt the other most brutally is usually an empty relationship, bereft of trust. Consider Sarah's story:

I was so hurt and angered by the discovery of my husband's affair that I did nothing for four days but cry. My face was puffy and raw. I couldn't hold food; my weight fell well below normal.

After those initial days—I refer to them now as days of mourning— I started to plot and scheme. I tried to think of the best way of getting back. Howard has a brother. He is two years younger; he and Howard have been competitive all their lives. I know his brother finds me attractive. He's even made passes at me. I decided to seduce him. It worked without a hitch; his brother was most cooperative.

Of course, when Howard found out, he felt as if someone had driven a truck through his stomach; he came home infuriated, but he managed to keep his cool. I immediately knew what was up and I walked into our older daughter's bedroom with her and closed the door. He came charging in and said to her, "Do you know what your mother did?" She replied, "Yes, she told me, and I'm glad because you're a son of a bitch, and if that made her feel better, you deserve it!"

That did it. He exploded; he was enraged. He pulled one of the wooden posts right off her bed and began smashing things. The room looked as if a bomb had exploded in it. I ran to call the police and he ripped the phone off the wall. He went insane. It was only then that I could feel compassion.

Sometimes the previously faithful partner may not flaunt the newly anointed affair. Merely knowing that "justice is being served" brings temporary relief. In other cases, the avenger subtly humiliates the spouse by conducting the illicit sex in such a way that the mate's friends and work associates know and the mate finds out through them. (This is what occurred with Sarah.) Still others disclose their retaliation by evidence left about the house, or scream it out in dramatic and frequently violent scenes.

None of these actions is productive; sometimes they even have tragic consequences. One man who had been unfaithful, when confronted with his partner's retaliation, committed suicide. In another case, a young secretary, who did not suspect that she was merely a weapon in a relationship war, killed herself when the affair was abruptly terminated.

Coping: Constructive Tactics

The least popular yet most constructive method of coping with the heightened emotions and broken trust at the discovery of an affair is to face it squarely and openly discuss the feelings and implications involved.

Dori and Alvin managed to do so. Here is how they began to communicate about his unfaithfulness:

ALVIN: *Dori, I am really bothered about the strain between us.*

DORI: *Did I start it?*

ALVIN: *Drop that for a minute. The point is we're both unhappy, and if we just continue to drag on with blaming and counter-blaming, it will end up in a divorce. If that happens there's no guarantee that either of us will be better off. A lot of men are worse than I am, and I still prefer you to any woman I know.*

DORI: *Thanks. I'll tell Florence Jackson that the next time I see her.*

ALVIN: (not being sucked into a destructive argument) *We have two children to consider. Their lives are also at stake here.*

DORI: *Does that scare you?*

ALVIN: *Yes, it does. I am concerned that we work this out for them as well as for ourselves. I want to tell you how I feel about what has happened. We really haven't talked about it yet, just around it.*

DORI: *A little psychology lecture coming up?*

ALVIN: *Maybe. Anyway, Dori, I feel very badly about what happened. I know you've been hurt and you're angry. I understand that I broke the trust between us. I want you to know that Florence really didn't mean that much to me; you've got it over her by a mile.*

DORI: *Oh, so you've come back to me on a rebound. Things didn't work out too well with Florence, is that it?*

ALVIN: *No. Things could have worked out, but I didn't want to split. I want to be with you.*

DORI: *I guess that's a compliment, in a backhand sort of way.*

ALVIN: *On top of feeling guilty about all that's happened, I get defensive every time the issue comes up; I even feel tense in anticipation of it coming up. I get mad and accuse you of a lot of things that are really petty; spreading the blame around a little, I guess.*

DORI: *Are you apologizing?* (Dori is beginning to change her reaction from sarcasm to sympathy in response to Alvin's persistent, honest, nondefensive stance.)

ALVIN: *I guess so. You know, I think, that this is difficult for me. I violated our trust and I am ashamed about that.*

DORI: *I know it is difficult for you. It should be! You betrayed me.*

ALVIN: *Your bitterness and bitchy attitude since you found out haven't made things any easier. It's hard to discuss your feelings if every time you open your mouth, you get walloped.* (Alvin is beginning to define the issues blocking their communication.)

DORI: (nondefensively) *How would you feel in my place? I felt humiliated and scared. Florence is five years younger than me; I felt as if I were being discarded for a newer model. I have felt old and ugly. Up to then I felt secure in our relationship.* (For the first time, Dori is revealing very personal, painful feelings directly.)

ALVIN: (softly, compassionately) *Why did you try to hide those feelings from me?*

DORI: *I felt so vulnerable; I was protecting myself. I didn't feel safe with you. I still don't trust you as before. I know you've been trying to reach me; I agree that my attitude has made it harder.*

ALVIN: *I understand more now of what's been going on inside you, Dori.*

In this dialogue, as contrasted with their earlier one, Alvin and Dori are less defensive, and more intent on honest expression. They are beginning to openly explore feelings about each other and about Alvin's breach of trust.

Several times Alvin could have been pulled into an angry, counterproductive argument. Rather than expressing her feelings and wants directly, Dori began by being hostile through sarcasm. Such attempts to lower the dignity and self-respect of a mate where there is intense anger and hurt are frequent. But it is self-defeating for the hurt person to hide feelings and "grin and bear it," or to use them as a manipulative tool against the other.

Here are some additional suggestions:

- There is a world of difference between a partner who openly states, "Hey, I'm hurting. Let's work this out," and one who demands, "You selfish bastard, you're hurting me! You have to stop!" The latter's blaming and demanding attitude provokes counterattacks and fails to promote understanding. Each conversation ends in a disruption; honest expression of feelings is lacking. Trust is not restored by these bouts, and the fighting is likely to continue until the relationship is torn apart or has seriously deteriorated.

- Since these encounters are so sensitive, the communication is likely to go nowhere unless one partner is able to stick to the problem at hand, that is, the hurt feelings, misunderstandings, and anger—as Alvin did (". . . the point is we're both unhappy"), even in the midst of blame-oriented messages ("Did I start it?"), such as Dori began with. By being understanding of Dori's feelings as well as honest about his own, and by forgoing the temptation to counterattack, Alvin was able to create an atmosphere in which Dori felt safe enough to express herself honestly. This is a beginning.

- Once emotions are directed toward the honest expression of feelings, examine what happened and its implications. Was the affair part of a larger pattern of mistrust and deception in the relationship? What can be done differently and more effectively so that trust can be strengthened? What are the hopes and expectations for the future? Very specifically, what kinds of behavior are acceptable and what kinds out of bounds? For example, some couples may wish to renegotiate their relationship agreement without restricting themselves to traditional sex-role expectations and definitions of fidelity. Others may feel strongly that conventional standards suit their emotional needs. Still others may differ bitterly and require professional intervention.

Other important areas of discussion include sexual satisfactions, the type of affair, and its meaning. If the sexual relationship isn't satisfactory, how can it be improved? What did the affair mean? Here's one possibility: The involved mate may say, "This was just a one-night stand. You are the one I love." Then the other may say, "Okay, I believe you." In these instances, trust and security may be restored by such simple measures as frequent reassurances of being loved and wanted, more frequent physical contact, cuddling, and fondling.

- If the affair was a serious love relationship, the wronged mate has a right to know where he or she stands—and rarely can be reassured quickly or easily. A shattered emotional investment of five, ten, twenty, or more years' duration is not easily repaired. It may be months or years before trust and a sense of security are reestablished. The relationship may never be the same. It is not unusual for the aggrieved partner secretly to open a separate bank account and take other actions to be financially protected in case of a recurrence or the dissolution of the relationship. This protective behavior may continue despite what looks like a healing of wounds and a repair of trust on the surface.

- One warning: Sometimes discussion of touchy issues can disrupt a relationship further by reopening old wounds (perhaps unfinished mistrust issues of the past) and heightening distress to intolerable levels. If this occurs, it is time to work with a person in one of the psychological professions. Therapy may help pace interaction at a manageable rate and guide it along constructive lines. Even therapy, however, will work only if both partners want it, if both will start to listen as well as talk, and if both will confront therapy issues openly rather than retreat into wounded silence or endless angry eruptions.

- An adulterous partner may act to restore the relationship yet the noninvolved partner continues to grieve for a long time. If so, the feelings of abandonment and rejection may have a deeper basis. They may be reacting to childhood hurts or betrayal. (Perhaps the father neglected his family for his work, or made promises that were often not kept, or the mother had no time to show love for her children or didn't provide an environment that was stable and predictable.) Or an old adolescent wound may have been reopened. (The distressed partner may be reacting again like after having been coolly cast aside by a high school sweetheart for a star athlete.) Persistent feelings like those can characterize an individual who has not developed a sense of self and of self-worth.

A developmental task of childhood involves moving beyond dependency on the parent. The same process must be repeated in the intimate partnerships of adulthood. If it is not, the discovery of an affair will be followed by unbearable and unceasing distress, and trust may never be restored adequately. In these instances, therapy is indicated.

The best antidote to persistent distress is growth toward autonomy and self-direction. This kind of personal strength can make a person more attractive to his or her partner and less susceptible to feelings of insecurity, depression, and anger. A discovered infidelity does not have to be a disaster; like nearly all emotional experiences, it presents an opportunity for movement toward maturity.

IN GUT  TRUST

Call it a hunch, insight, inspiration, gut feeling or inner voice. Whatever you call it, intuition is a powerful tool at your command if you are able to tap into it. And make no mistake about it, intuition is intimately tied to trust, in this case trusting your own inner messages. Paying attention to your intuitive sense can help with trust by

- strengthening your confidence and belief in yourself and your judgment;
- providing you with insights and feelings about your partner, thereby assisting your efforts to assess trustworthiness; and
- bringing additional awareness to the fore that is ordinarily overlooked in resolving trust dilemmas.

Consider the following examples of people who sensed what was going on, likely to happen, or what to do, because they were in touch with and trusted their inner experience:

- Alicia had a bad feeling about a new business partner that her husband Dan brought to dinner. Dan was excited about expanding his jewelry manufacturing company and he talked eagerly about the financial expertise and marketing know-how that his new partner Jerry would bring to the company.

Yet as Dan spoke, Alicia looked at Jerry and just had a "bad feeling." Something in her gut told her that Jerry couldn't be trusted and when she told Dan later that night, he just laughed at her.

A year later, Dan wasn't laughing when he discovered that Jerry had siphoned nearly half a million dollars from the company, enough to almost put him out of business.

- Susan had a romance with a dashing man she met during her summer vacation. Fernando had been traveling in the United States from Brazil and told her of his plans to relocate and find a job in her city. He made her feel special with his concern and attentiveness, and spoke of marriage. Susan was smitten by his charm and sensitivity, yet a part of her held back. Her friends were impressed with Fernando and pushed her to become more involved with him. However, something about him that she could not put into words caused her to resist.

A few days after a friend urged her to take him up on his offer to return to Brazil to meet his family, he was arrested and charged with smuggling drugs. He was eventually convicted and sent to prison.

- Alex had a sense something was very wrong when his wife Pam returned home from work. On the surface she was her usual bubbly self as they shared their experiences of the day over dinner. Yet his gut told him something was wrong.

Later that night, when he shared his feeling with Pam and probed more deeply, she finally acknowledged there was a problem she hadn't wanted to tell him about. Her mother had been diagnosed with cancer, and she was trying to be stoic, not wanting to bring any more pressure to bear on Alex, since he was undergoing a career transition.

Once Alex heard about the medical problem, he was readily supportive. The experience also helped to reinforce Alex's sense of trust in his gut instinct.

How did these people know? They just had a strong feeling that something wasn't right. Call it "vibes," a "warning signal," whatever, something deeply intuitive gave them a sense of foreboding and they knew to trust it, even if others did not. As these examples illustrate, intuition allows you to pick up cues that may otherwise be overlooked.

Laurie Nadel, author of *Sixth Sense,* says it well. According to her, intuition is a form of "knowing without knowing how you know." It's like having a satellite dish in your brain that enables you to pick up information, which comes to you in the form of "images, ideas, impressions, and feelings." It's an immediate knowing about something without the usual process of reason or conscious thought to evaluate the information.

How Does This Inner Knowing Work?

Our rational, pragmatic, and fact-oriented culture tends to downplay the power of intuition, dismissing it as a form of superstition and delusion. Yet this kind of knowing actually has long been part of human intelligence. Indeed, it has actually contributed to the survival of the human species. As psychologist Daniel Cappon observes, "Intuition most likely has its origins in ancestral instincts for survival and adaptation. There is no way that our human ancestors could have survived without intuition. There could not have been much conscious thinking before speech evolved, some 250,000 years ago."

In other words, if our early human ancestors were making their way through a clearing and some fearsome animal was nearby, they had to sense the danger and escape its jaws. There was a need to respond instantaneously in perilous times, without any hesitation or doubt. Much later, the human ability to speak and reason evolved, and the mind developed barriers or censors to enable us to think logically without the interference of intuitive chatter. Yet, there are times when these barriers recede or become porous like teabags, such as when we dream and unconscious images bubble up. When we get sudden insights, like the sense that our partner is tempted to begin an affair despite fervent denials, this may be an example of the intuitive process.

In the view of Cappon and many other scientists, intuition derives from ancestral human instincts that make us more sensitive to our surroundings and the people in it. In the course of human evolution, survival instincts have been transformed into intuition. It is a signal that comes from deep within the brain. We react instinctively to this quiet warning, if only we respect it and listen.

Increasingly, researchers studying intuition have recognized the power of this inner feeling. For example, creative artists commonly find their source of creativity in their intuition, while many of the most successful business executives report they use their gut feelings to make major decisions, even after they have gathered all the facts. Albert Einstein, the world-renowned physicist who gave us the formula for how energy works in the universe, acknowledged that he was intuitive. And many Nobel Prize winners in science, such as Linus Pauling and Jonas Salk, respect their hunches. When Cappon interviewed them, they told him: "Of course, we have hunches. We know the answer before we work it out."

So how does this intuitive process work? How do we get hunches and inner insights? Our brains are divided into three separate parts. One is our reptilian brain, which creates the patterns we observe and our everyday habits. The second is the limbic system, which is the source of our moods and emotions. And the third is the neocortex, which is divided into a right hemisphere that sees holistically, and a left hemisphere that responds in a linear, logical way. According to *Sixth Sense* author Laurie Nadel, an intuitive response starts in the right hemisphere, which signals the limbic system—giving a feeling or emotional sensation and a physical reaction. You might get a visual image from the right hemisphere (such as when an image flashes of someone you know is going to call) or a verbal signal from your left hemisphere (such as when you hear a warning like "Watch out. He's no good!").

In short, all of these parts of your brain work together instantly to give you this inner awareness and knowing. If you are able to pick through the clutter of thoughts and feelings that conceal insight, you can gain valuable information about whether to trust someone and how to respond to a threatening situation.

Developing Your Intuitive Abilities

Like any ability, intuitive abilities vary, with some people more in touch with their inner knowing than others. To some extent, women are more intuitive than men, because a larger network of fibers links the right and left hemispheres in female brains. Consequently, an insight that arises in the right hemisphere spreads more rapidly to other parts of the brain. Men have strong intuitive feelings as well, though they may prefer to call them "hunches" and "gut feelings."

Then, too, researchers have found other differences between men and women. Women tend to be faster to sense a problem in a relationship, often before overt signs of difficulty show up. On the other hand, men are more likely to use their intuition to solve problems, since they are more result-oriented. Another difference may be that women and men don't get the same signs. According to Nadel, a woman feels a warmth in her chest as a warning signal, while a man feels his stomach or diaphragm tighten.

Putting the Pieces Together

In either case, an insight often stems from your ability to recognize patterns based on experience. You synthesize the bits and pieces of knowledge you have gained. Thus, if women pay more attention to relationships generally, they will likely be more insightful about this, while men who pay more attention to work issues will experience more intuitive flashes in solving problems.

We can increase over time our ability to synthesize and gain insights. Each of us can become more intuitive by paying more attention to the intuitive flashes we get. We thus enhance our experience and confidence in recognizing patterns, which is the way experts develop expertise. Indeed, as Milton Fisher reports in his book *Intuition,* that's what several researchers studying intuition found, among them Nobel laureate Herbert Simon, a psychology professor at Carnegie Mellon University, and Robert Glaser, a psychology professor at the University of Pittsburgh. Intuitive awareness comes quickly when we are knowledgeable about a particular area, whether it's molecular biology or our partner. We just know things in a global holistic way, without having to think about them consciously, because these facts have combined together in a pattern.

Insightful thinking may occur whenever you become knowledgeable in something. As researchers have observed, the way people think and reason changes as they learn more about something, such as learning to play tennis. Initially, you may think about it in an analytical, step-by-step way. But as you become more familiar with it, you begin to combine information into clusters that form patterns. Consequently, you no longer have to go through steps, since the cluster of information is readily available. In fact, the process moves so quickly that most often the insight gained is right there for you, as when a professional tennis player anticipates where the ball will be placed.

Recognizing How Intuitive You Are

To develop your intuition, it helps to know your baseline, your starting point. To begin the process, consider the skills involved. Intuition isn't just a matter of perception and awareness. Psychologist Daniel Cappon, who developed the IQ2 test to measure intuition, asserts that a number of different skills actually make up the general ability. Each of us has a combination of different skills. It helps to assess how well you do in each area, so that you can better use your stronger skills and develop the others.

According to Cappon, intuitive skills range from the lower-level *perceptual* ("input") skills, through higher-level *ideational* ("output") skills, to the highest level, where you can bring uncommon but accurate meaning to images.

With lower-level perceptual skills, you absorb information. Cappon describes them as "latent and passive," or "just there." They come into play when, for example, you are relaxing in bed and close your eyes and see the image of your lover float into your mind's eye. You don't do anything to generate it; it just appears.

Assuming all is well in your relationship, such images will usually be positive and supportive. If you have images or feelings associated with them that concern you, such as seeing your lover flirting at work, your perceptual abilities are in effect speaking to you.

At the next level are ideational skills, which are triggered in response to some situation or stimulus. Something sparks your imagination. The "something" can be a cloud, a flower in your garden, a passerby on the street. This is the process that psychologists use when they present you with an inkblot and ask you what you see in the blotches, or in other tests where they show you a variety of pictures and ask you to make up stories about them.

At the highest level is the ability to find meaning in the images produced through perception or ideation. That's when, for example, you suddenly visualize yourself and your partner having a fight when everything seems to be going fine, and you realize there are hidden issues you have been afraid to bring up before. The imagery makes you aware it is time to raise these issues that have been bothering you.

More specifically, Cappon divides the three levels of skills into categories:

Perceptual (Input) Skills

1. *Perceiving quickly.* You recognize something with only a short exposure. This is essentially the subliminal effect, which tunes you into a quick flash that passes through your mind. If you can increase your ability to notice these flashes, you can access this information from your intuition.

2. *Perceiving with a limited amount of definition.* You can identify something even though it is unclear, unfocused, or otherwise obscured, regardless of whether it flashes by or you have more of an opportunity to view it. In a sense, this is your ability to fill in the missing pieces, similar to doing a jigsaw puzzle. Again, as you are better able to do this, you will gain more complete insights.

3. *Recognizing something in a mass of other information.* For example, you are able to find Waldo in a picture with many other figures. You can distinguish what's relevant from the perceptual clutter. The same process occurs as you are lying in bed and you attend to the critical message from the dozens of reflections passing by your mind's eye.

4. *Making distinctions when you perceive several things one after the other.* An example of this is when you see a series of images in a psychological test and are asked what you see. It is the ability you use when a stream of the day's activities flashes by your mind as images and you sort out the important elements.

5. *Recognizing what isn't there.* For example, you go into a room and notice that something is missing. The same skill can be applied to images that flash by in your mind.

6. *Seeing all of the parts as a "Gestalt" or whole.* For instance, you notice how all of the trees make a forest. The same skill applies to mental images.

7. *Registering the flow of time correctly.* For instance, you know you have been on the phone for three minutes, look at the clock, and it confirms that you have been.

8. *Noticing not only the whole scene, but also specific details of it.* For instance, you drive by a group of people on the street, see each person individually, and are able to identify details about them as well.

To evaluate your perceptual intuitive abilities, think about how well you do perceiving in the areas above. Ask yourself which ones you do best and which ones are deficient. You can improve in those areas you are deficient by creating little exercises for yourself. For instance, imagine yourself as a camera, take a picture in your mind's eye, and write down all the things you see.

Ideational (Output) Skills

1. *Your active imagination* involves looking at something which triggers your imagination to produce images. To get you thinking about your relationship, try looking at a picture or object associated with you and your partner and see what associations are triggered. If the images are positive ones, that's a sign all is well; if you associate to other kinds of images that raise trust questions, this could be a signal to pay closer attention to your relationship.

2. *Anticipating or looking ahead* is, for example, when you sense a friend will call or when you know you will get a letter from someone who hasn't written in a long time. You can use this skill to anticipate twists and turns in your relationship.

3. *Your sense of timing* guides you to do things at an opportune moment. Some investors, for example, are good at knowing when to buy or sell stock. Likewise, you may be good at knowing when it's best to bring up a difficult topic for discussion and when to hold back.

4. *Coming up with good hunches* that are used to solve a problem, sometimes even before you consciously think about the problem. When you are good at coming up with hunches, your solutions are correct or work well. For example, if you sense there might be a problem in getting your partner to visit with relatives, you can come up with responses to any objections before they are voiced.

5. *Coming up with the best method for acting on your hunch.* If you're known as a good problem solver, that's a sign you have good intuitive skills in this area. What's more, this skill demonstrates that your hunch was productive; you are proving it is correct.

6. *Being able to understand the causes or reasons for something by empathizing or identifying with others.* This intuitive skill permits you to put yourself in the place of others to understand why they have acted as they have. In a relationship it is quite advantageous to see the world through the eyes of your partner, including how your partner views your behavior. It's an ideal skill for helping you feel closer to your partner, and it also helps you assess how your partner is thinking or feeling if you have problems leading you to fight or distance yourselves from each other. When you perceive what is going on for your partner, you are in a better position to respond effectively.

Interpretive (Meaning-Making) Skills

1. *Determining what's appropriate,* which involves looking at a situation or mass of information and deciding what's really

important. For instance, you may hear a lot of rumors and conflicting stories about something that your partner is doing. This ability helps you sort through the confusion to the heart of the matter.

2. *Seeing the meanings of things,* such as divining what an object or event symbolizes. In relationships, partners may drop subtle hints or behave in ways that are suggestive. Picking up those cues is one use of this intuitive skill. For example, a woman left an inexpensive pen in a man's office, he called her and joked that she must have wanted him to contact her. After a pause she laughed and acknowledged that she had. She left the pen *because* it was disposable, giving her suitor the opportunity to call only if he were interested.

Together, all of these skills—perceptual, ideational, and interpretive—combine to make up intuition. Breaking down the components of intuition allows you to consider one aspect at a time and improve upon it. All of these skills can be refined. Indeed, when Cappon used his IQ2 test to assess intuition, he found that just by taking the test, people were able to improve their ability to be intuitive. By becoming sensitive to their abilities, they were challenged to do better.

Though you may not take the test yourself, you can still think about each area of intuition and consider how well you do. Rate yourself from 1–5 in each area, which will give you a general sense of how well you do. Afterwards you can decide what areas you want to work on improving.

How Do You Know When You Know?

But how do you know when your intuition is correct? How do you know when your gut feeling or the images you see are really coming from intuition? Certainty about knowing is one of the trickiest abilities to acquire when you use your intuition, since you can easily be influenced by outside factors and be wrong. Your own wishes and fears can also mislead you.

For example, you sense your partner is not being totally straight with you, but then you realize that what your partner said reminded you of the way an old boyfriend used to lie to you. In another instance, your intuition tells you that something terrible is going to happen if you and your partner go to your sister's wedding. But then you realize you are uneasy about going because you don't want to see your obnoxious brother-in-law.

Your intuition is like that, elusive, not usually as clear as a San Diego afternoon. You get little signs, symbols, images, and impressions, which may be meaningful, or may not. Thus it becomes important to know when you really know, and really don't. In *The Empowered Mind: How to Harness the Creative Force Within You* and in *Mind Power: Picture Your Way to Success in Business*, sociologist Gini Graham Scott deals with just this question.

As she points out, even if you lack absolute certainty, you can still get a strong sense of whether your information or choice is right, by measuring your *impression* of the intensity of your belief and your *sense* of the probabilities of being correct.

For example, ask yourself, on a scale of 0–100, how strongly do I believe what I believe, and see what number flashes into your mind. Or ask yourself, on a scale of 0–100, how probable is the choice I am making the right one and see what number comes to mind. If your response is high, 70 or more, you feel reasonably confident what you believe is true, or that you are making the right decision. If it's 90 or higher, you feel nearly certain about what you are doing. If you get a medium or weak response, perhaps you need to reevaluate your belief or decision.

In making this assessment, you are adding a level of review that gives you a little remove from your initial response. The review helps you double-check or reconfirm your experience; it's like getting a second opinion.

You can also increase your confidence by testing the strength of your belief or the certainty of your decision against the outcome. Verifying the accuracy of your feelings about future events or recalling how you felt in the past when you were correct will help you recognize an accurate signal, since you will become familiar with the sensation.

This approach isn't foolproof, since it is based on subjective feelings, impressions, and beliefs. However, it is a helpful way to attune to your gut feelings and keep track of your accuracy.

Julie's experience illustrates gaining confidence from following intuition. Her partner was moving to the East Coast due to a job offer. Julie was trying to decide whether she should go also or stay where she was. Feeling restless where she was, she was drawn to follow her partner to a place that might offer more opportunity. And maybe they would get married if the relationship continued to go well. But should she really pull up her roots?

A week after her partner suggested the move, she went to a retreat where people were encouraged to think about where they were going. In an exercise, she saw herself living in a house on a hill by the ocean, although it wasn't clear where it was. Significantly, however, she was there by herself, not with her partner. She returned from the workshop feeling uncertain, since the image seemed to be telling her that she would move—but that her partner would not be part of the picture.

A few days later, her employer told her of a promotional opportunity that would take her to Los Angeles. Her experience at the workshop encouraged her to at least look into the offer. After she went to Los Angeles for an interview, she learned that her employer would be providing her with a rental house for the first six months and, yes, it was right on the ocean, looking very much like the house in her vision.

Considering all the factors, including her intuitive experience, she decided to accept the promotion and turn down her partner's offer to go East. She felt that with the passage of time she could reassess whether she wanted to continue their relationship. However, after several months, when at her new job she met the man she eventually married, she was more certain than ever that she had done the right thing in listening to her intuition.

Julie's experience provided her with more trust in her sense of knowing, especially since the outcome was so positive. It was a lesson in heeding that deep inner sense of knowing we all sometimes have.

Boosting Your Intuitive Confidence

A key factor in intuition is being able to distinguish the quality and intensity of your feelings when you are correct from those when you are not. How? By paying close attention to how you feel in both cases and noticing the differences, you can compare current feelings, premonitions, and beliefs to past patterns, using that as a guide. Again, since intuition is subjective, there are no guarantees, but awareness of past results will increase your chance of correctly evaluating a hunch.

The following exercise, adapted from *The Empowered Mind* by Gini Graham Scott, will help you look back and notice the differences. It works well if you have someone read it to you, or make a tape of the exercise and play it back as a guided experience. (Alternatively, after you read the exercise, get relaxed and give yourself the instructions with your conscious mind using self-talk. Then, let your receptive mind respond to your instructions. This method can be difficult, unless you have had practice working with meditation and guided imagery.)

INTUITION EXERCISE

Assessing Your Feelings and Insights

(Time: About 10–15 minutes)

To start looking at the differences in the way you feel when your intuitive impressions are correct and when they are not, first relax. Concentrate on your breathing for about a minute. Notice it going in and out, in and out, in and out.

Now think back to a time when you had a strong feeling, premonition, or belief about something that you didn't consciously know about but that later turned out to be *correct*. Maybe you had a feeling about what someone was *really* like ... Maybe you had a premonition of some danger ahead ... Maybe you believed something about someone that later turned out to be true. Whatever it was, focus on this incident and see it happening right now. See it on the screen in your mind and watch ...

Now, recall the feeling you had about this event before it happened. What did it feel like? Feel that feeling now. And pay attention to how it feels ...

How intense is this feeling? If you were rating it on a scale of 0 to 100, how intense would it be? See a number flash into your mind.

Also, notice where this feeling is located. Is it in your head? Your heart or chest area? Your stomach or solar plexus? All over?

Are any images or words associated with that feeling? Any pictures? Any voices? Any memories? If so, what are they like? Now, let go of that feeling and that incident . . .

Now think back to a time when you had a feeling, premonition, or belief about something you didn't consciously know and that later turned out to be *incorrect.* Maybe you thought you knew what someone was *really* like . . . Maybe you had a premonition of some danger ahead but there was no real danger . . . Maybe you believed something about someone that later turned out to be false. Whatever it was, focus on this incident and see it happening right now. See it on the screen in your mind and watch . . .

Now, recall the feeling you had about this event before you discovered you were wrong. What did it feel like? Feel that feeling now. Pay attention to how it feels . . .

How intense is the feeling? If you were rating it on a scale of 0 to 100, how intense would it be? See a number flash into your mind.

Where is this feeling located? In your head? Your heart or chest? Your stomach or solar plexus? All over?

Are any images or words associated with that feeling? Any pictures? Any voices? Any memories? If so, what are they like?

Is there anything about the feeling that is a signal that your intuition is not correct? Is there something about its intensity, its location, the images or words associated with it that might be a cue to ignore this feeling? Now, let go of the feeling and the incident.

Finally, reflect on the differences you just experienced in the intensity and quality of the feelings you had when you were correct and when you were incorrect. How were they different in their intensity?

In the location of the feeling? In the images or words associated with them? Those differences are cues you can use in the future to tell you whether or not to pay attention to a feeling, premonition, or belief.

Tracking Your Intuition

Another way to improve your intuition success rate is to practice using your intuition in everyday situations. Notice the difference in the way you feel when you are correct and when you are not, and keep a mental or written record of how well you do. Over time, you will increase your ability to sense when your intuition is correct.

For example, you can get immediate feedback on whether your intuition is right or wrong by trying to determine:

- the number of calls on your answering machine when you return home;
- the number of letters you will receive in the mail;
- whether a certain person will call;
- whether someone will cancel an appointment; or
- whether someone will be at a certain event.

The possibilities are endless. You can test yourself with just about anything, though it is best to start with less important situations. As you test yourself, notice how certain you felt and how accurate your impressions really were. Over time, both may go up. As you feel more certain about your ability, you can apply it to making decisions and setting a course of action in situations that really matter.

9

TO BE, OR NOT TO BE, VULNERABLE

The Struggle with Vulnerability

The word *vulnerable* is derived from the Latin, "vulnerare," to wound. *Vulnerable* literally means "able to be wounded." Commonly we use the word when we're feeling weak, fragile, and emotionally worn down. No wonder most of us want nothing to do with vulnerability!

Beginning in childhood we learn to protect ourselves against emotional attacks from those around us—family members, peers, and teachers. What's more, if our parents are guarded and closed, they serve as role models for exercising emotional caution. The old adage, "Don't show too much of yourself because *they* will use it against you," becomes part of our unwritten life rules. The sad fact is that people tend to feel ashamed or embarrassed to directly acknowledge their needs for love and intimacy.

Indeed, appearing or being vulnerable does have drawbacks. If politicians show the slightest sign of weakness—and vulnerability is often equated with weakness—it can destroy their career. A consultant trying to close a major business deal must give the impression of absolute confidence, or risk losing the client. Most surgeons do not express self-doubt in the face of a frightened patient; they often foster the impression of being superhuman.

In relationships, most of us proceed with caution. Vulnerability, even with those closest to us, is often perceived as dangerous. Communicating in an intimate manner can be terrifying because it places us in the risky position of being susceptible to rejection or humiliation. This outcome is an ever present possibility because exposing our needs may threaten others who are struggling to ignore their own needs.

Depending on the extent that we protect ourselves, we may experience a sense of safety, yet feel alone and isolated. It is not surprising that couples learn, usually over a period of years, to eliminate conversation that touches on areas of sensitivity and conflict. Sometimes they do it so well that relatively little remains for them to talk about.

Is the answer simply to wear your heart on your sleeve? It's not that simple. Vulnerability, like many factors in relationships, is not without its complications. Too much vulnerability and you burst into tears if your partner brushes your sleeve without saying "excuse me." Yet, without some degree of vulnerability, intimate relating and life itself are devoid of meaning. The capacity to suffer along with a loved one as well as to be open to your own pain and disappointment is a crucial component of a healthy relationship. It's a matter of balance.

In its most destructive form, vulnerability produces not only self-pity but also self-doubt and blame. For example, Carol, a thirty-nine-year-old executive, suffered a devastating loss of confidence when her husband left her for her best friend. She put on thirty-five pounds, doubted her judgment, began slipping at work, and secluded herself. "If I'd been so wrong about my husband and my best friend," she said, "how could I hope to be right about anything or anyone?"

While vulnerability does involve exposure and risk, it is also an opportunity for deeper self-awareness. It enables us to see and understand things we ignore when everything in a relationship is going smoothly. For one woman, the vulnerability produced by a cancer scare led to a shake-up in her relationship. "Basically, my lover simply disappeared," she said, adding:

> *During the week I waited for the biopsy results, he wasn't there for me. He reappeared after I was told the tissue sample was benign. But what if it hadn't been? He told me he wasn't good in dealing with illness; I told him I wasn't good in dealing with cowardice—*

and we split. The experience taught me I need a real partner, not just a playmate. The feeling of being exposed during that week of waiting was horrible, but it forced me to open my eyes.

Vulnerability. Without it, our relationships are sterile; with too much, emotion runs rampant, making closeness impossible. Here, then, are the ingredients that combine to give and get the best of vulnerability in a love partnership.

Acceptance

We all need opportunities to let our hair down, to be weak, to be sad, to be childish, to be silly. We seek to do this with someone with whom we feel safe. The wish to be accepted is a matter of wanting our feelings to be acknowledged and respected. Psychologist Abraham Maslow referred to this as the basic need to belong—the desire to feel accepted without needing to prove ourselves or demonstrate our worth through obedience, cleverness, or accomplishments.

It is especially critical to experience acceptance as children. During the dependency of childhood, when we are most impressionable, negative messages have their most dramatic effects. As Steven, a highly skilled physician, said about his relationship with his father:

It was bad enough being teased, but he really discouraged me when he'd say things to my mother like, "This kid will never be anything. He will always be mediocre. He just doesn't have what it takes." I was only six the first time I heard that and I really got upset.

Nothing I ever did was good enough in his eyes. One day, I finally said to him, "Dad, why are you always picking on me?" He said, "I'm not picking on you. I'm just trying to push you to do your best. Can't you see that?" I guess I couldn't see it and after medical school and a six-year surgical residency I still don't.

All I know is that I find a way to feel inferior no matter what I accomplish. People think that just because I'm a surgeon I must have a great opinion of myself. That's just not true. I'm supersensitive to almost everything that anybody says to me. I can't take anything at face value. I always think someone's down on me. I think my wife's down on me, I think my patients are down on me. I sometimes lie awake at night thinking about what people said to me during the day . . . and I read criticism into everything.

I know that my arrogant manner is really a cover for the insecurity I feel practically all the time. This is how I hide my mistrust of other people; I try to protect myself from further hurt by keeping them at a distance.

As Steven's statement shows, the wish to be accepted follows us into adulthood and goes well beyond love relationships. Consider the typical social encounter where many of us are busily trying to get people to like us, or maneuvering to display what we think are our strengths while concealing what we believe to be weaknesses. Becoming preoccupied with a hidden agenda to gain people's acceptance or approval, we often neglect to simply enjoy being with them in a natural, effortless, unpretentious way.

Or consider chance encounters. Have you ever met someone and right away felt antagonistic without being able to pin down anything that sparked your reaction? Often it is a subtle sense of negative judgment that you are picking up, conveyed by voice inflection, gesture, body posture, or other nonverbal means. Verbalized or not, critical judgments create an environment hostile to trust and vulnerability. The tendency is to become combative and defensive with such people, or to withdraw from them.

In contrast, you have met persons with whom you felt instantly comfortable and at ease. At the time you may not have fully comprehended why you felt good. It is often because you sensed the other person's ability to like and accept you as you are. That is precisely what most of us yearn for with a lover. If it is largely deficient, vulnerability is kept in check and trust cannot fully develop.

Relationships that do not provide the type of sanctuary in which you can "be yourself" are sometimes those in which lovers view each other as one-sided or in an idealized way, so that acting "out of character" is quickly suppressed. An example: Arnold doesn't acknowledge Pam's existence unless she behaves in a certain manner. The desired behavior has not been explicitly defined, although Pam knows that what Arnold wants—"an undemanding woman who takes care of his needs and remains pleasant"—isn't always how she feels. When Pam is needy, and not so pleasant, she is subtly and sometimes not so subtly told by Arnold, "You're mistaken. That's not really you. I'll ignore it and it will pass. Soon the real you will return." Pam feels that her lover's acceptance of her is very conditional, which has limited her ability to trust him more fully.

In some instances, intolerance and nonacceptance go beyond denying or discounting part of an intimate's being, and instead take the form of a direct attack at a sensitive area. Nina and Don are both in their early thirties and have been married for eight years. Nina is pregnant with their second child, and they are planning to move from their apartment into a house. Don is hardworking and earnest; however, as a young consulting engineer with little business experience, he has suffered some serious financial setbacks.

NINA: *That house in Lakeside is perfect for us. The location is first-class. We'll be making a great investment.*

DON: *It does have lots of nice qualities, but I'm afraid that the asking price, combined with the taxes in that area, makes it out of reach for us.*

NINA: *Well, have you seen something that is more affordable?*

DON: *Yes, the houses in Davisport are larger, the taxes are lower, and the prices are within reason.*

NINA: *Are you kidding? That area is nowhere. Who would want to live there?*

DON: *What do you mean? We both grew up there. It's a solid, stable, middle-class area with good schools and services.*

NINA: (beginning the attack) *We could easily have afforded the house in Lakeside if your consulting firm hadn't collapsed.*

DON: *Oh, Nina, don't rub it in.*

NINA: *If you were competitive, you would not have lost so many potential clients to other firms. Now you seem to have given up. Working for someone else isn't going to produce any real money.*

DON: *I admit I made a few mistakes—that's why I'm learning more about the business. Listen, Nina, I feel bad enough . . .*

NINA: *A few mistakes? Hell, am I to be tied to a third-rate flunky who can't even hold a business together, who can't even provide a nice home for his family?*

DON: *Davisport homes are nice . . .*

NINA: *Look, we're going to buy the house in Lakeside. I'll ask my father for the money. I'll explain to him how you've made mistakes and that sort of thing; he'll loan us enough for a large down payment, and then even you will be able to keep up with the mortgage expenses.*

DON: *Nina, you know it's important to me not to take money from your parents. You've done this before, disregarding my feelings; we'll take the house in Lakeside, I'll pick up some freelance work in the evenings to cover the extra cost.*

NINA: (having effectively crushed Don) *I knew you would work it out. I'll call the real estate agent and make the arrangements.*

Individuals like Nina castigate their partners or make harsh judgments if they do not conform to an exacting standard. They are not likely to promote trust and make vulnerability safe. Indeed, when one partner looks at another like King Pygmalion, with a view toward making him or her into something new and different, guardedness will probably be engendered on both parts, at least eventually.

In striking contrast is the individual who is self-accepting and consequently has the strength and understanding to tolerate the foibles of another. Keith, a forty-eight-year-old high school English teacher, was fortunate to become involved with such a person. He had been divorced three months when he met Helen, a woman with whom he developed a stormy but ultimately positive relationship:

At the time I met Helen, one of my strongest and most persistent feelings was pain—not just emotional pain but actual physical pain: nausea, headaches, and the like. I remember saying once that when my wife left me for another man and I lost the connection to my family—

it was as if a knife were put into me and turned around each day to cut up my insides.

My first reaction to Helen was one of surprise at her sensitivity and awareness of what and how I was feeling, even when I expressed it inarticulately or hardly at all. Then I began to get the feeling that not only was she sensitive but that she also cared for me.

It seems crazy, but I fought desperately against this. I was firmly convinced that to give in to her acceptance of me meant selling my soul; there would be a high price for being vulnerable with another person. Hey, I was still reeling from the last time I yielded.

I tried demonstrating to her how unworthy I was—how selfish, inadequate, nasty. I tried hating and attacking her. I told her that she couldn't possibly think well of me, that I was defective. I suggested that she was being deceitful and cruel to pretend that she accepted me.

But she was always there, treating me with respect; she was a firm, strong pillar that I beat on to no avail and that merely said, "You are a worthwhile human being." She saw past my bullshit, yet she didn't condemn me for it.

Not that she was a saint; she expressed outrage and frustration. She engaged me and fought ferociously, but she always did so in a way that didn't belittle me. Her words were strong yet soft; somehow the sharp edges were removed.

She conveyed that I was not an obnoxious person but a person acting in an obnoxious manner. In other words, I was not disqualified and considered garbage because of my difficulties.

As I look back on it now, I was putting all my faults and inadequacies on the line so that I could be done with the process of rejection. And Helen calmly—and sometimes not calmly at all—by her acceptance of me as a person, peeled off my armor layer by layer. Slowly, it became clear that it was safe; I realized that I could give my trust to Helen and that I could handle the vulnerability.

That sounds like a simple kind of experience, yet I have found it so freeing, being able to trust somebody on a deep level, the feeling is awesome. I feel elevated, more accepting not only of myself, but also of others. In my relationships with other people, I try to see them as struggling with the same things as I do, not as adversaries or enemies.

As was the case with Keith, feeling uncertain about our own accept-ability or worth accounts for much of the antagonism and conflict that leads to mistrust and guardedness. When we inwardly view ourselves as inferior or undeserving, we often compensate by blaming, criticizing, or verbally attacking others as a way of bolstering our sagging self-regard.

However, acceptance is not the same thing as indulgence. We may not agree with all the actions of another person, but by acceptance we acknowledge and respect the fact that he or she is still worthwhile. It is an attitude that expresses "I may not tolerate some of your behavior patterns, but that doesn't make you less of a person."

Relationship partners who are willing to reach out to each other in this manner address differences without condemning each other. They are wise to the human struggle, so when their partner behaves nega-tively, they attempt to understand the basis for the action. Emotional safety then permits vulnerability.

Self-Disclosure

Perhaps the most reliable way to feel trust is when we allow ourselves to be known by being open about feelings and thoughts. Revealing ourselves—our failings as well as our successes, our quirks and our interests, our likes and dislikes, our less than endearing qualities as well as our strong, likable ones—is conducive to a trusting love relation-ship. When our partner shares genuine thoughts and feelings, and when our questions are answered truthfully and without reserve, this inspires trust.

While we may not always like what we hear, knowing where we stand in relation to a partner is usually preferable to being left guessing. Secretive or closed people may present themselves as an interesting challenge, but with the passing of time not knowing what they feel or think about significant personal issues creates distance.

Although self-disclosing is important, most of us find it difficult. We've learned to guard our vulnerability as a result of past hurts, real or imagined. Hidden behind our caution is often the belief, conscious or implicit, that to be one's real self is dangerous, that exposure of feelings and thoughts will lead to being unwanted: "If people found out what I was really like, they wouldn't want any part of me."

Christine described such a dilemma—how confused and empty she had become regarding her own convictions:

During elementary school I had fantasies of being accepted by girls I admired, but I never approached them. I selected my friends from those who approached me and usually felt at least a little ill at ease with them.

In high school I was considered shy; I was aware of those guys I really wanted to know yet I would form relationships with guys who were not my first choice. I also continued to play it safe by not revealing too much of myself.

I still experience a tension when I'm with other people. I'm more relaxed by myself. I realized recently that when I'm alone I don't have to perform; this accounts for the reduction in tension.

Over the years I have developed a knack for determining what kind of woman a guy likes and then playing the role. Even if this pleases the guy, it creates a tension within me; since they have an inaccurate concept of me, I am left with the burden of maintaining the pretense.

When I'm in a social situation, a party for instance, I could be lively and appear to be having a good time but all the while I'd be putting on a little drama, creating the illusion that I'm bright and interesting so that guys will see me as attractive. I am always aware of being judged; it is very important for me to gain the approval of a guy I admire. Sometimes I even surprise myself by taking positions that I don't really feel, if I think that would please a guy I want to impress.

It's been so long since I stood up for my convictions that I don't know what I feel or what my beliefs really are. I haven't been honestly myself. "Be yourself" I hear people say. It sounds easy but it's not. I don't know what my real self is; I've lost touch with that.

One of the few times that I allowed myself to be off guard, I couldn't handle it. I was involved in a heated discussion and my face was flushed, my tone communicated anger, and I was shaking my finger at this guy—my boyfriend at the time. Yet when he said, "Well, let's not get angry about this," I replied with sincerity and surprise, "I'm not angry! I don't have any feeling about this at all! I was just pointing out the logical facts."

He looked at me. Seeing my obvious anger he broke out in laughter at my statement and I was utterly embarrassed. My defensiveness, my unwillingness to accept myself kept me from being aware of my anger at the moment. I realized later that I was terribly angry at that guy, even though at the time I was convinced I wasn't.

Maybe the day will come when I'll have attained a strong enough sense of self-trust that I'll allow someone into my heart with the confidence that I won't evaporate or something if things don't go well. I know I have a lot of work to do before that day arrives.

Christine knows that her behavior and even her feelings do not flow naturally from her genuine reactions, but are a facade behind which she has been hiding. She is discovering how much of her life is guided by what she thinks she *should be* rather than by what she *is*. Still more disturbing, she recognizes that she exists in response to the demands of others, especially men, that she seems to have no direction of her own.

Frequently, when a partner relates in a limited or contrived manner, it influences us to wonder what he or she really feels or thinks. Consequently, we tend to be wary and cautious; uncertainty leaves us feeling insecure; we are not quite sure where we stand in the relationship.

In contrast to guardedness, open interpersonal behavior in the long run feels secure; it is trust promoting. Consider a small child who has not been compromised by a limiting environment. If the child expresses affection or anger or contentment or fear, there is no doubt in our minds that he or she "is" the experience, all the way through. The child is transparently fearful, or loving, or angry; there is no deception, no pretense. (Perhaps that genuineness is why so many people respond warmly to small children—we feel we know exactly where we stand with them.)

Of course by the time most of us have reached adulthood, many factors have contaminated the process of self-disclosure. For one thing, many middle-aged adults today grew up in a household in which openness between their parents was not even an aspired goal. Deceptions and lies are almost institutionalized, standard operating procedures between the sexes. As a result, rather than sharing the closeness of a love relationship, many women and men live in separate emotional worlds.

A lifetime of inattentiveness to feelings is strikingly demonstrated by Martin, a musician, and Gloria, his wife of twenty years. Two months before this conversation, Gloria had discovered Martin's infidelity.

MARTIN: *I don't think we've ever been a team intimately. I've never felt close to you. I always felt you were holding back. I loved you with reservation, the same reservation I imagined you had in not revealing yourself to me. I don't think either of us really felt safe enough to do that.*

THERAPIST: *Gloria, how did you feel about the relationship all these years?*

GLORIA: *How did I feel? Well . . . I suppose lonely. I wanted to be with Martin more. I wanted to be more passionate and open with him, less reserved, more vulnerable, but I always felt he wanted me up on a pedestal. I stayed there to keep him. I didn't trust that the "real me" was good enough for him.*

MARTIN: (stunned) *But Gloria, I never knew that. Why didn't you tell me how you felt? Why didn't you say something?*

GLORIA: *Afraid, I guess. You never asked. I thought that was the way you wanted things.*

THERAPIST: *Martin, how come you never said anything?*

MARTIN: (crying) *For the same reason, I suppose. I took it for granted that Gloria was happy with the status quo. I didn't want to hurt her or be hurt myself. God, I wish I had known how you felt back then, Gloria. I didn't really want to see other women. I wanted to be closer with you but we just didn't make each other safe enough for that. That bothers me; it bothers me a lot.*

The waste of time, energy, and potential happiness is appalling. Through the years of Martin and Gloria's marriage, what they both really wanted was so much more similar than what they each supposed the other wanted! This same kind of waste affects millions of relationships. A main cause is the failure of lovers to be attuned to each other's feelings.

While vulnerability is usually trust-promoting, some people, more often women, go over the top with it. To them, the right partner is that special someone who will reveal a magical depth of spiritual communion, with intense discussions about their deepest feelings. Unfortunately, this idyllic picture of a soul mate is hard for some women to give up. Consequently, they are forever being "betrayed."

And while some partners complain that they want more openness, they may not always be receptive when it occurs. One man, Ernesto, had this to say:

> *I own my own business, and whenever I would share the problems I was having, my wife would tell me how it was all my fault that I was having problems. She was getting angry, and it wasn't as if my business or my business problems was the only thing I spoke about. I'm not one of those narrowly focused guys, talking only of business and sports, nor do I put in unreasonable hours or conduct myself irresponsibly. Her attitude really confused me.*
>
> *Finally I said to her, "I see you don't want to deal with the problems I'm having at work. I'm not going to tell you anything anymore." Her reaction was even more confusing. She was insulted that I didn't want to talk to her about work anymore.*
>
> *And then one day we were talking and she admitted that she couldn't handle it. She really didn't want to hear about my struggle. She really didn't want to know. She told me she just wanted to hear that everything was just great and the money was flowing in. Otherwise, she said, she felt insecure, and that made her angry.*
>
> *She told me this as a kind of confession, and I appreciated her honesty but where does that leave me? Who do I talk to?*

Good question—should Ernesto persist, or keep his business problems to himself? Can being too open erode trust? And what factors should be considered before broaching sensitive issues?

As a general rule, honesty and disclosure is the best policy for promoting trust. However, other factors must be considered, such as timing, interest of the other person, appropriateness, and the effect of the disclosures on either participant. One research study reported by psychologist P. W. Cozby found that of the two least liked and least trusted members of a work setting, one was the most secretive and undisclosing, and the other was the highest discloser in the group.

Both too much and too little disclosure may be associated with mistrust, while some intermediate amount—under the right conditions and expressed with sensitivity toward the listener—seems to promote trust. But most of us, especially men, are not in danger of being too disclosing. Rather, our problem is being too protective, not permitting enough vulnerability.

Direct Expression

"We're not communicating" is the classic complaint in many love relationships. Actually, in relating to another person it is impossible not to communicate. Words can be used to hurt, calm, nurture, confuse, anger, provoke, deceive, dominate, manipulate—the list is endless. Even silence conveys a message.

Communication in relationships is a constant. The way one behaves, moves, and gestures all transmit messages. However, sometimes the meaning of a message is hard to decipher. This is most true when trust is not strongly established, for then indirectness and subtlety play a major role.

Janet and Dan have been married three years. When Dan was still married to his first wife, he had an affair with Janet, who was divorced. Although Dan and Janet were intrigued by their brief encounter (it happened during one of Dan's business trips), it was not pursued at the time because of Dan's marriage. Two months later, Dan's wife left him for another man. Six months after that, Dan and Janet were married.

Dan regards his infidelity in his previous marriage as an exception, viewing the motivation behind it as desperation. His marriage had been deteriorating for a long time, and he acted quite out of character. He operates from a standpoint of fidelity and trust with Janet.

Janet, in turn, is guided by mistrust and suspicion: "If he did it to his previous wife, he can do it to me." Consequently, their discussions about absences from home, particularly business trips, are filled with confusion:

> JANET: *You know what, I think I'll go to Chicago with you, Dan. Maybe I can be of some help to you there.*
>
> DAN: *That's okay, Jan. I'm provided with a nice hotel room, meals, transportation, and so on. I don't really need any help.*
>
> JANET: (disappointed) *Oh, then I can keep you company.*

DAN: (starting to feel vague unease) *Jan, it's nice of you to want to be with me, but my schedule keeps me busy from nine in the morning to midnight; and since it wouldn't be appropriate for you to sit in on business meetings, I would hardly see you.*

JANET: (persistent, with a trace of annoyance in her voice) *I think I'd like to go anyway.*

DAN: (with impatience and annoyance) *Listen, the company won't pay your way, and I would hardly see you, so there's no point in our spending an extra eight hundred dollars that we can ill afford for nothing. Let's leave it at that.*

JANET: *Let's not leave it at that. I'm going!*

DAN: (angry and frustrated) *Shit! Janet, for Christ's sake, when you get so damned unreasonable, I feel as if I don't know you anymore. You're not like the woman I married.*

JANET: (her anxiety and mistrust escalating) *That's it! You don't want to be with me anymore. I knew it! You're looking for someone else.*

Conversations based on indirectness and private, untested assumptions such as Janet and Dan's are usually symptomatic of underlying trust issues. In this instance, Dan isn't sure what's going on, maybe Janet is simply being stubborn. Janet assumes Dan is up to something—another woman, specifically—and is being purposely evasive. Had she directly stated her concern or had Dan asked why the trip was so important, the outcome might have been different. These patterns of behavior are somewhat present in almost all relationships. Sometimes an argument's source is unclear or camouflaged. After many futile bouts the result is often you-hurt-me-so-I'll-hurt-you. Vindictiveness can then become a major force in the gradual escalation of mistrust.

As the mistrust created by indirectness increases, it spills over into other areas of the relationship. Once a negative, suspicious atmosphere has been established, more indirectness and guardedness are likely to follow as protection against the "enemy." For example, Janet may begin to attack Dan on any number of lesser issues: his dress, his manners, his parenting, and so on. In actuality, Janet's criticisms are related to some-- thing entirely different: she is insecure about losing Dan. In reaction to her seemingly unprovoked criticisms, Dan becomes guarded and defen- sive. Then Janet grows more suspicious and less willing to expose her vulnerability by speaking to her concerns.

The Spiral of Indirectness

In couples therapy one frequently sees both partners caught in a futile push-pull based on indirectly expressed concerns. For instance, a woman may have the impression that her man is not open enough for her to know where she stands with him, what is going on in his head, and what he is doing when he is away from home. Quite naturally, she will attempt to make herself more secure by asking him questions, watching his behavior, and checking on him in a variety of other ways. He is likely to consider her behavior intrusive and react by withholding from her information that in and of itself would be quite harmless and irrelevant, "just to teach her that I am not a child in need of checking."

Rather than making her back down, her partner's reaction increases her insecurity and provides further fuel for her worries and distrust: "If he does not talk to me about the little things, he must be hiding some- thing." The less information he gives her, the more persistently will she seek it; and the more she seeks it, the less he will give her.

It is not long before the drama becomes like two sailors hanging out of either side of a boat in order to steady it; the more one leans over- board, the more the other has to hang out to compensate for the insta- bility created by the other's attempts at stabilizing the boat, while the boat itself would be quite steady if not for the insecurities of its pas- sengers. Unless something changes in this situation, unless the couple discusses its assumptions openly and explicitly, the occupants of the boat—the relationship—will be under constant undue strain or, worse yet, finish up in the water.

A direct and pointed statement by one of the partners may not in fact resolve an underlying trust issue. It may, however, result in an admission that indeed there is a problem. That's a beginning.

Read My Mind

Yet another type of indirectness that fosters confusion and mistrust is the *disguised request.* Consider: A couple has just come out of the water after a delightful moonlit swim. The woman says, "Let's go inside. I'm sleepy." The man responds, "It's nice out here. Why don't we lie and rest here?" The woman, angry, storms into the house. The man, equally angry in response to her abrupt departure, drives off to a local bar. What happened?

The woman, by saying she was "sleepy," was actually signaling her desire to make love in the house. The man, ironically, was signaling his desire to make love in the moonlight. In an effort to guard against feeling vulnerable, neither directly said what each wanted, and both felt rejected by the other. The evening ended in anger and hurt rather than in pleasure. Preventing this unfortunate turn of events may have been as simple as saying, "Let's go inside. I'm in the mood to make love" or "It's nice out here. Why don't we make love in the moonlight?"

Often we don't want to take responsibility for our requests, so we hide and disguise them in questions, hints, obscure suggestions, and countless other manipulations, all in an effort to satisfy our desires without the risk of being rejected.

The problem with disguised requests, as with all indirect messages, is that those that are not understood are not likely to be satisfied. Consequently, they promote resentment and a false sense of betrayal in the requester, while fostering mistrust and confusion in the responder.

The Power of Vulnerability

Vulnerability, as we have seen, has many faces. Here are some suggestions for staying emotionally open, even under trying circumstances:

- *Own your own issues.* Stop blaming your partner for your mistakes, bad behavior, problems with your family of origin. These are your problems, your issues, and your solutions to find. For example, Joan was convinced that her husband was hopelessly insensitive and that all their marital problems resulted from his selfishness. She missed no opportunity to tell him just that. After a painful separation followed by much reflection, she began to own up to her side of the problem. Never having experienced a father who was emotionally available, she had been wanting her husband to be the "good parent" she never had—one who was always selflessly attentive to her needs. Of course, he could never fulfill such fantasies and eventually became involved with another woman as an escape from his confusion and discouragement. It wasn't until Joan openly discussed her part in their conflicts that their differences were reconciled.

- *Resist the temptation to be defensive.* For example, your partner pokes fun at you about your weight. Consider something like, "I feel hurt when you joke about my weight. People have kidded me about it all my life and it's become a sensitive topic." This statement is a simple description of how you feel. It also offers information that may assist the other person in understanding how past experiences have contributed to your present feeling. (It does not counterattack by asserting, "Well, you're not exactly Slim Jim!" It does not cast responsibility away from you and it does not pose threats like "If you don't stop, you'll be sorry!" All of these statements are manipulations intended to coerce another person to change behavior. It rarely works over the long run and it masks your vulnerability.) Stick to your feelings and stand by them, whether or not they are received favorably.

- *Notice your evasions.* Keep a small notebook with you each day for a full week; jot down each and every one, no matter how petty (for example, complimenting someone falsely, smiling when you're actually annoyed, telling people what they want to hear). Study the notebook at the end of each day to determine patterns of inauthenticity. Share these deceptions with your partner and make a commitment to gradually change your behavior, to be more open, more vulnerable.

- *Share the worst stories.* Consider the thoughts and experiences about which you are most ashamed or embarrassed. Pretend someone else has confessed these things to you. What counsel would you offer that person? Are you more benevolent toward this "other person" than toward yourself? Demonstrate confidence in your partner by talking about one or more of these experiences.

- *Stop judging your partner.* Focus on expressing how you feel rather than on the nearly impossible task of trying to change your partner's behavior. By doing this, you shift from the usual nagging and attack. In so doing, you are leaving it open for your partner to voluntarily respond sensitively and in an accommodating manner. Simply share how you feel in response to your partner's words or actions without pressure or threat. For people who care about one another, self-revealing communication can be very compelling. In fact, some studies suggest that when a person risks being vulnerable, empathy is an innate human response.

- *Seek integrity.* Using self-revealing statements to sensitively share your feelings may appear to reduce you to a weaker position in terms of getting what you want from your relationship. It may seem that fighting for change is the stronger and more effective strategy. In reality, the opposite is true. There is a hidden power in vulnerability—it does not equal weakness. A special kind of inner strength is summoned when genuine feelings are asserted rather than blaming, attacking, moralizing, and other manipulations. Even if your partner is not responsive, you are more likely to respect the integrity of your own expression. In contrast, angry, accusatory growls typically camouflage a host of fears or areas within yourself that you have yet to understand, or accept.

- *Don't push your partner away.* Make it conducive for your partner to move toward you. Stress can bring couples together, but it can also lead to withdrawal or smothering. When your life is stressful, be supportive without smothering, and don't respond to withdrawal by pulling back yourself. Under stress, if you can't regulate your emotions, control your behavior. Don't make things harder than they need to be. Try to keep perspective.

- Lastly, to trust another person, you must have trust in yourself. If you can count on your inner strength, you will be more willing to risk the vulnerability that comes with trusting others. Discuss your fears of vulnerability with your partner.

Following the guidelines above will assist in providing the strength and courage to love well; to muster the courage to be vulnerable without feeling overwhelmed.

RESTORING **10** TRUST

Taking Responsibility

Trust may begin as a leap of faith, but ultimately it is not a gift; it must be earned. Communicating is always important, but it is critical when there has been a violation. Specific conversations must occur in order to mend a broken trust. As the offending partner, we especially need to demonstrate through unmistakable effort that we are committed and it is emotionally safe to be intimate with us.

In a time of emotional crisis it is not easy to talk productively, but it is essential. What's more, the emotional fallout from a broken trust is not usually limited to the offended partner. The offender may also feel badly. Feeling distressed, one may openly validate the offended partner's feelings, thereby clearing the way for the breach to be repaired. This is an admirable response but, unfortunately, not very common. More often, the partner who has violated trust reacts defensively, adding insult to injury. Now the offended partner not only feels hurt and anger, but the sense of betrayal is heightened by denial, distortion, or minimizing.

Rather than heal the wound of betrayal, the lack of openness by the offender will almost surely erode the trust-base further. The couple will inevitably move toward increased and unproductive conflict, either over the areas involved in the source of mistrust, or over a wide range of lesser issues.

The point is that there are two main ways for the offender (and the offended) to make things worse when confronted with a trust violation: one is withdrawal, to keep everything bottled up inside; the other is to erupt, to emote without restraint. If you are having too many conversations with yourself, you are probably not having enough with your partner. If you are screaming, hurling insults, and looking to vent without concern for the impact, then the relationship will deteriorate.

Here are some guidelines for constructive discussion:

- *Stay on focus.* It's not fair to dredge up mistakes made twenty years ago or to complain about how much the in-laws are hated. A fight is not an opportunity to rehash old grievances. Stick to the issue at hand or else the discussion will surely sink from the weight of the problems.
- *Define issues.* Be clear and specific about the problem. This will help you stay on track.
- *Listen—really listen.* Don't just pause until it's your turn to speak again, with your mind formulating the next sentences while your partner talks.
- *Don't interrupt.* You can be angry without being rude or bullying.
- *Don't personalize.* Stay with the issue rather than attack the person. Contending that your partner betrayed you in some manner is legitimate; name-calling, belittling remarks or other verbal assaults are not constructive.
- *Recognize "his" and "her" conflict styles.* Men and women have different conflict styles as well as intimacy styles. Respect the differences. A male may, for example, feel emotionally flooded and need a time-out. A woman may well view it as withdrawal. If he reassures her that he is simply taking a few minutes to "regroup," she is likely to abide.

Bear in mind: the trust-breaker, as reassurance that the efforts to restore trust are sincere, must be willing to look inward, confront the personal issues that lead to trust breaches, and acknowledge them openly and responsibly.

To begin, an unequivocal apology is in order. No excuses, no "buts," no extenuating circumstances. The apology is something like, "I am very sorry that I behaved in an irresponsible manner, that I betrayed your faith in me by deceiving you." It is not something like, "I'm sorry you're upset about my gambling but if you didn't make me so nervous about money I wouldn't have taken such risks to pay the bills."

The former approach is the way that adults talk who realize that they are in charge of their lives, and the consequences of their actions. The latter is the way that children talk who believe that they are victims of other people or circumstances. Unless they change their view and begin to take charge of their lives, the chances that they will be trustworthy partners are near zero.

Following an apology is the discussion, or more likely a series of discussions with the goal of understanding the basis for trust violations. Simply stated, "Why has this happened, and what is going to happen that will prevent a recurrence?" Understanding the basis for a breach of trust does not guarantee that it won't happen again. However, unless there is a belief in magic, it is unreasonable to assume that trust violations will not recur without addressing the reasons they have already occurred.

Some questions to pose for a discussion: What is your understanding of why this (these) trust violation(s) occur? What influences from your family of origin may be undermining your relationship? How can I trust that you will be trustworthy in the future? What changes need to be made in the relationship to strengthen the trust and intimacy? Very specifically, what kinds of behaviors are acceptable and which are out of bounds? Can the damage be repaired? What will it take? What are the hopes and expectations for the future?

Resolving an Impasse

Trust violations are at times clear cut with a readily identified offender and offended. But many instances are more complex and do not lend themselves to easy assignment of responsibility. When trust is damaged not by specific actions but by chronic misunderstandings and unrecognized differences, both partners will typically experience themselves as victims. Each will feel upset and bewildered by the other's inability or refusal to acknowledge how she or he feels.

The following statements may characterize the attitude underlying the impasse:

> *"If you treated me as though you really love me, I would feel emotionally safe with you."*
>
> *"If you felt emotionally safe with me, I could really show my love."*

> *"If you would only make me feel welcome, I'd be home all the time and I'd be loving."*
>
> *"If you stopped disappearing for hours at a time and you were more accountable, I wouldn't act so nasty."*

> *"If only you didn't drink so much, I wouldn't be so suspicious of you."*
>
> *"If only you weren't so mistrustful, I wouldn't feel so bad and drink so much."*

> *"If you'd hold my hand and pay attention to me at parties, I'm sure I'd never flirt again."*
>
> *"If only you weren't such a flirt at parties, I wouldn't have to compete for your attention."*

Who is to take the initiative? Usually, each is willing to change but waiting for the other to make the first move.

In these instances, whether conflict is overt or passive (in the form of withdrawal), the relationship comes to an impasse. Neither party can see or validate the other's side. Discussion becomes the "dialogue of the deaf" so familiar to couples therapists.

An effective antidote to an impasse is the Emotional Conference. Make a fifteen-minute date for a meeting at the same time each week. The agenda is feelings. Each partner spends five minutes talking about the emotional impact of the other's actions. The actions may have occurred at any time during the course of the relationship, all the way back to the first date.

The speaker begins by briefly describing the incident and then describing the emotional impact. This is *not* a gripe session; it is an intimacy builder. The speakers are talking about their own feelings, the listeners are getting to know how their partner responds emotionally, and more about their partner's vulnerability. After each partner's five minutes, the listener takes a couple of minutes to mirror what the speaker said.

The few simple rules are:

- Use "I" statements. (You are talking about your feelings, not casting blame on the other person.)
- Absolutely no interruptions.
- After the speaker is done, the listener summarizes the major points—without editing, analyzing, interpreting, or judging.
- Each person should have a separate agenda. (The second partner doesn't get to rebut what the first person said. Otherwise the conference degenerates into one asking, "How could you see it that way?" and the other countering, "Why don't you see it the way I do?")

What is the point of the Emotional Conference? It is hoped that both partners will consider how their actions affect each other, learn to listen attentively, and reveal themselves, vulnerability and all. The experience is also a weekly reminder that no two people, even the long and happily married, view incidents and actions in exactly the same way. This is an excellent way to soften the impasse when neither partner is willing to validate the other's experience about confusing trust issues.

Andy, thirty-nine, and Ruth, thirty-four, had been in a relationship for six years. They found that they were accusing each other of minor trust violations, such as not calling when promised, telling "white" lies, and using personal disclosures in later arguments to hurt the other person.

In the early weeks of the Emotional Conference, they would interrupt each other, challenge each other's "inaccuracies," and begin "innocent" discussion afterward that erupted into arguments. After a couple of months, the tension between them had softened and Andy felt safe enough to tell Ruth he was under a lot of stress at work. He realized he was taking it out on her in an effort to brace himself in the event she was disappointed in him for not advancing in his career. He feared lack of success would diminish him in her eyes because he'd secretly struggled with inferiority feelings all his life.

Ruth neither offered comfort, nor editorialized. "I hear you saying that you fear losing my regard for you if your career doesn't go well," she said. "Your testiness with me had been a way of distancing yourself in the event of a disappointment."

In another conference, Andy's candor encouraged Ruth to talk about her strong desire to be viewed as compellingly attractive in Andy's eyes, and to tell him how she tries to hide her flaws in fear he would lose his interest in her. "Sometimes," she said, "if I think you're viewing me negatively, I get defensive and pick on you for no real reason."

"The conferences didn't have an immediate impact on our relationship," Andy says, "but slowly it brought us closer. Our trust issues eventually stopped coming up. Both of us became more relaxed, more open and secure about our commitment."

The Emotional Conference is not limited to couples who are at an impasse in their trust issues. It is a powerful tool that can and should be used by any couple attempting to repair intimacy and trust. It should occur once a week but in circumstances where the issues have accumulated over time, doing it more often may be warranted.

Behavioral Changes, General and Specific

While talking is critical, it is not enough. Behavioral patterns require change as well. In the past, for example, the partner who has violated the trust may have come home at night, barely mumbled a hello while reviewing the mail, made some small talk during dinner and retired to the TV for the remainder of the evening. That routine—not much of a relationship promoter under any circumstance—definitely won't cut it in the wake of a breach of trust.

As the offending partner, we need to think through exactly what we'd like to see happen in the relationship and behave in a manner that promotes our vision. Regardless of the specifics, the general message our behavior should convey is, "I love you. You matter to me. I want to demonstrate that I am trustworthy." This may require a shift in the usual manner of behaving and in the daily routine; it can be a lot of work, a real stretch for some people. But if a serious trust issue is to be repaired, that can only happen in the context of a caring environment. *It is up to the offending partner to create a caring atmosphere, even if it is at some sacrifice.*

The reparative behaviors required do not have to be sensational. Indeed, some people are so preoccupied with major shifts that opportunities for small but important gestures are overlooked. Even though a base hit would have been possible, these individuals value only a home run and usually strike out.

Others mistakenly believe that a repair process moves along on its own energy and consequently do not bother to fuel it at all. These individuals seem to sidestep escalating conflict by sweeping the incident under the rug and acting as if it hadn't occurred. It may appear as if conflict has been safely avoided in these instances. Appearances notwithstanding, there is no avoidance of trust violations without consequences.

When one or both partners fail to acknowledge and address a trust violation, the conflict has simply gone underground and practically always results in gradual withdrawal from the relationship. It is not unusual for this to evolve into an eventual separation that leaves one or both partners confused as to its basis.

While some individuals avoid the issue altogether, still others show their concern in a manner that is inappropriate. "I don't think he cares that I don't consider him trustworthy . . . he certainly doesn't show it if he does," Susan comments about her husband Gary. She and Gary have been married ten years, and on at least a half-dozen occasions he has broken his word, lied, or otherwise let her down. Gary expresses his remorse in practical, "sensible" ways: Instead of talking things out, which he sees no point to, he brings home a new kitchen gadget; rather than phoning from the office, he works straight through and often quite late, hoping to earn a promotion. To Gary these are "make up" behaviors; to Susan they have little to do with building her confidence in his trustworthiness.

This may be one situation where the Golden Rule, "Do unto others as you would have them do unto you," is not the right approach. Gary believes that he is acting in a loving, trust-building manner. In reality he is behaving in an insensitive, even selfish manner ("If it pleases me, it should please you."). If Susan were to state that this is not what she wants, Gary might well become insulted and defensively reply, "I was only trying to make things better between us."

George is an excellent cook. He does the shopping and prepares elaborate, rich meals ever since his wife, Diane, discovered he was having an affair with a colleague at his office. He considers his preparations his way of making up for the heartache he caused. Diane, however, is getting fatter by the month, her blood pressure is skyrocketing, and she is unhappy with herself. She tries to diet, especially since she found out about George's dalliance, but George makes it more difficult when he puts a hurt look on his face and explains how he spent the entire morning preparing the chocolate mousse she is refusing.

Is George's behavior simply misguided benevolence? Actually, George seems to be nurturing his own ego, upstaging Diane with his fancy preparations, encouraging her to feel less attractive; his "restorative" behavior is more likely one-upmanship, selfishness, and lack of consideration. Rather than genuinely repairing a broken trust, he is making himself feel good at Diane's expense while assuring himself that she won't retaliate with an affair of her own because she will be self-conscious about her weight.

Such behavior appears to be caring but is really selfish or what might be called *pseudobenevolent*. Consider, too, the spouse who is greeted effusively at the door upon his return from work by a wife who, despite her promises, habitually overspends. She fusses over him and relaxes him with a drink (he abhors the taste of alcohol) despite his insistence that he relaxes best by having a few moments of solitude. Or the husband who never keeps his word but each time makes it up with a gift, usually something his wife doesn't care for, but he adores. Then there's the protective partner who "makes up" for a betrayal by constantly asking, "Are you all right?" and "Is everything OK?" Brief separations are infused with telephone calls, faxes, reminders to take this or that, all of which drive the recipient to distraction. Once again, if the goal is to please and help a love partner heal, the behaviors must be sensitive.

Just as everyday relationship-supporting behaviors usually need to be strengthened, trust-specific requirements must also be considered.

First of all, the trust-violating behavior in question must stop completely. No more contact with a lover, for example. One must do whatever it takes to give up drugs or alcohol, including detox, recovery meetings, and inpatient treatment, as needed.

A common request is for greater accountability. Especially in instances where there has been an affair or uncontrolled gambling or substance abuse, accountability may involve an accurate itinerary during travel, calls during the day, and coming home from work in time to have dinner with the family.

In addition to accountability, most trust-damaged lovers require much greater consistency and reliability. Being clear about intentions and keeping agreements, even those that seem minor such as calling when promised, are very important. Once the trust wound has been exposed, sensitivity is increased and must be respected. Some couples transfer assets into the offended partner's name, making available monthly bank statements, credit card statements, and phone bills. Other couples insist on therapy, with a complete and detailed description of the trust violations. Still others need some time for intimate talk and reassurance each day.

The specific requests vary from person to person, but in all cases they should be in the service of helping the hurt partner feel more cared for, appreciated, and emotionally secure. And that's how the trust-breaking partner should view them, rather than as punitive and arbitrary.

The Role of the Betrayed

Strengthening trust is not a one-person endeavor. The offended partner shares in the responsibility of the repair process. In fact, if there isn't receptiveness to the possibility of trusting again, and an encouragement of the offender's efforts to restore confidence, the process is destined to failure. An "indefinite sentence" or a prolonged period of coldness and alienation, perhaps going on for months, will almost surely result in the offended partner giving up efforts to reconnect. It is most helpful, in contrast, to consider carefully what is needed to restore trust, spell it out (not globally, like "be more reliable," but specifically, like, "call when you say you will") and give the offender a blueprint for making amends.

Realistically, it is a major challenge to be responsive to an offending partner's efforts when there has been a betrayal or pattern of deception. In these instances, the negative cycle is well established and will not yield easily; simply thinking about the relationship differently, although important, is not powerful enough. More is needed. Here the As-If Principle, described by the philosopher Hans Vaihinger in 1877, is a useful strategy.

The As-If Principle is based on the notion that changing your beliefs about a person (including yourself) is best accomplished by acting *as if* the change has already been achieved. Noted psychologist George Kelly, among others, reported great success with this approach. Dr. Kelly encouraged his clients to act as if they did not have the problem that distressed them. The shy college student, for example, was instructed to act as if he were self-assured when he approached girls on campus, and the critical husband was asked to act toward his wife as if her behavior were acceptable.

Assuming that the skills are available (e.g., knowing how to act in a self-assured way) and the emotion (e.g., fear or anger) is not unusually intense, acting *as if* creates an opening to go beyond the past. It allows old prejudices to be dispelled through reality testing. Even a bumbling effort at first, if viewed liberally as a move in the right direction, initiates a new vision, provides a glimmer of what could be.

This same principle is fundamental to all relationship restorative efforts. Commonly, for example, distressed partners complain that the violated trust has resulted in a loss of love feelings. Not feeling loving, they do not respond to acts of love. And herein lies the stalemate: Feelings of love will not magically grow; they can only be remedied through loving interaction with a partner. Therefore, the key to revitalizing the relationship is to act *as if* you feel loving; only then do you increase the chances of stimulating your own love feelings, as well as your partner's continued initiative. *Love is an effect of loving behavior.*

In brief, the sequence is do something to feel something rather than wait to feel something in order to do something. Every time you do something, the feelings and ideas consistent with that behavior are reinforced. It's as though the act recharges the feelings and beliefs that coincide with it. Thus, if you distrust someone, your being disparaging and hurtful will increase your feelings of alienation. Conversely, if you want to increase your acceptance of another person, offer criticism sparingly and compassionately, and respond encouragingly to their reparative efforts.

Of course, it is not likely that you can make yourself feel trusting toward someone who has repeatedly betrayed you simply by being responsive to yet another attempt to get on your good side. But a weakened trust can be strengthened by acting *as if*—by encouraging the offender's trust-building efforts, even if your feelings aren't quite behind it yet.

Carl calls his wife at work and apologizes once again for lying to her about a credit card purchase he made after they had agreed to a moratorium on the use of plastic. Beth, his wife, doesn't excuse his behavior, and in fact is tempted to take the opportunity to lambaste him (again). Instead she thanks him for calling. She tells him she appreciates his reaching out since he knew she was worried about their precarious financial status as well as shaken by his broken promise.

It took courage for Carl to call. He did so fully expecting Beth would beat up on him; when she did not, he was grateful and then he felt even more motivated to restore her confidence in him.

To avoid pitfalls, here are a number of suggestions:

- *Be behavioral.* Although feelings and beliefs are vital for the repair of trust, neither carries the impact reserved for action. Telling a partner of your love does not have the immediacy and potency of a demonstration. It is what you do rather than what you profess that will ultimately make the difference.
- *Be gradual.* Many attempts at repair and change fail because they are too sweeping in nature. Attempts to change a relationship too quickly or too greatly in too short a period of time are responsible for much disillusionment and despair. For example, rather than making all requests at once, which may be overwhelming, consider making them gradually.
- *Expect resistance.* Compounding the difficulty we all have with change is the risk of moving closer to another person. While we

want the rewards of closeness, many of us fear the increased vulnerability that accompanies intimacy.

- *Be persistent.* Both parties can be expected to test the sincerity of each other's change efforts. Testing may take the form of provocation, questioning motives ("You're doing this only because you're afraid I'll leave you") in an attempt to discount the change effort, expressing feelings of hopelessness ("These changes are just too artificial and trivial"), or a return to earlier behaviors. By viewing testing as a natural part of the change process and continuing with the restorative behavior despite temporary discouragement, a new precedent is set.

- *Be positive.* It is much easier to increase positive behavior than it is to directly stop negative behavior. For example, rather than spotlighting a halt to excessive criticism, you are more likely to get results if you focus on a response incompatible with criticism—namely, an increase in appreciative comments. Behavioral science research suggests that undesirable behavior is more effectively controlled in this manner.

Self-Soothing

When both partners are committed to repairing a broken trust, many obstacles can be overcome so long as there is a respect for the identity, equality, and integrity of each other. Sometimes, however, a person who has been betrayed receives little or no support from the offending party and is left to heal alone.

Betrayal calls upon you to draw from your inner resources in order to avoid choking off emotions and hardening into a cynical bitter person. Before you can learn from the experience and move forward, a period of grieving is often necessary. Supportive friends may be invaluable during this time, but ultimately the healing will be up to you.

In any event, the first principle of healing is the empowerment of you, the hurt partner. While it may not seem fair, you must take charge of the healing process. Taking charge involves turning inward and accessing your own resources to regain your emotional balance. This is called *self-soothing,* your ability to comfort and care for yourself without self-indulgence.

Self-soothing is not becoming heartless or cold-hearted; it is taking better care of your own heart. It does not involve tantrums, whining, self-pity, or bingeing on food, drink, or drugs. It does involve taking care of yourself while you're not getting along with your partner. Self-soothing permits you to quiet and calm yourself. The process requires that you not give up on yourself, nor tell yourself it is too hard to settle your emotions down. It may be hard, but not too hard. You have to stick with yourself, just as you would with a friend going through a difficult time.

Here are some specific suggestions for soothing yourself:

- As much as possible, reduce the number and complexity of tasks you face by notifying others, including your children, to temporarily make fewer demands. Postpone anything optional that adds to a hectic, pressured schedule. An ailing psyche, like an ailing body, requires special attention and energy until it is strengthened.

- Attempt to do less together and enjoy it more—rather than the reverse. You may have to reduce or break off contact with your partner to self-repair when interaction is consistently too unsettling. How much physical separation, and for how long? That depends on your emotional state: How badly are you feeling? How quickly can you recover from contact? Make it clear to your partner that your time-out is for self-repair, not withdrawal.

- Do your best to stop the negative mental tapes. Stop "awfulizing" the situation or telling yourself, "How could [my partner] do this!" Accept the present reality and settle down. Quiet yourself instead of getting more worked up and losing perspective.

- If you can't regulate your emotions, control your behavior. Once again, try to regain some perspective, as reactions and situations don't last forever. Behave in a productive manner that you'll respect afterwards, even if your emotions suggest otherwise. In other words, ask yourself, "If I felt better, how would I handle this?" Then, do your best to approximate that behavior. In contrast, when you start saying, "Maybe I

shouldn't do that, but . . ." or "Maybe I shouldn't say that
but . . ." take your own advice!

- Give your trust difficulties purpose and meaning by recognizing how you may have played a part in the problem, and also
how these issues may confront you in the future. If you don't
see the part you may have played in the trust conflict, keep
searching. A law of physics states that every action has an equal
and opposing reaction; correspondingly, every relationship
problem involves *two* people. For example, there can be no
dominating husband without a submissive wife, no interrupting
wife without a passive husband. Every "villain" requires a cooperative "victim." Consequently, when discussing or thinking
about the problem, it is good policy to consider your own role
as well as your partner's.

Do not expect the suggestions above to be easily or quickly soothing. When the wound is deep, the greatest trap is to expect too much
healing to happen too soon. Again, fortify yourself on the nourishment that friends and your own interests provide, as you navigate
these distressing and uncertain times.

When to Consider Bailing Out

Healing from a trust betrayal or a pattern of violations is a slow
process. Some people feel it could take a lifetime, maybe longer. And
they may be right. The process of healing, especially when the violation has been serious and piercing, unfolds ever so slowly and continues throughout your relationship. There's no end point, no time you
can say it isn't even a memory. Though healing is difficult, a legitimate
and concerted effort on the part of both partners is often sufficient for
the relationship to mend.

However, there comes a time in some relationships when the memory
of joy is so distant, and the possibility of its revival so improbable, that
parting appears more reasonable than pain and loneliness without end.

Other instances may be like an individual with a life-threatening illness: vital signs may be weak but their very existence is a signal for
hope. When emotional pain is great, it is sometimes difficult to judge
when to continue and when to give up and move on.

The critical question becomes, when is the trust repair process not working? When should one call it quits, or consider a separation or divorce? No easily applied guideline exists, because intimacy is too complex a process to fit specific formulas. Some general observations, however, may apply:

- Typically when the trust repair process has broken down, one or more factors are present: an unwillingness to acknowledge and probe the meaning of trust violations, continuing deception, an unwillingness to communicate openly, and an inability or unwillingness to empathize. Usually there is a lack of respect in the relationship, one or both partners no longer feels emotionally safe and is unable to recover that feeling despite real effort over a reasonable period of time and therapy with a competent professional.
- Trust problems are probably not being resolved when you feel that you can function better without, rather than with, your partner. It is not working when you would usually rather be alone or with somebody else other than with your partner. It is not working when you think your children would benefit from the absence of your partner. A repair process has not worked when there is no fun in the relationship.
- Typical signs of recovery include beginning to feel calmer and more accepting of yourself, improved concentration, improved mood, feeling more at ease with your partner, feeling more energetic, and experiencing pleasure to the degree you had before the problems began. In addition, two helpful signs of healing are becoming more interested in the present and the future than in the past, and being more apt to approach the relationship with eagerness than with fear.

When, then, should a couple wisely consider parting? Partners should not make a decision based on what family and friends think, social appearances, or convenience. In most cases, a married couple should not consider divorce without professional consultation. Is it clear that you two are only functioning together with severe physical or emotional harm to one or both? And that the damage is irreversible—or reversible only with an effort that is not forthcoming from both partners?

If so, then consider divorce. Consider it the best way to ensure your sanity and, especially, that of your children. As difficult as divorce is on children, youngsters are usually better off with divorced parents than in a crazy-making family.

Unfortunately, many couples caught in an irreversible and mutually destructive relationship do not end it. They persist, despite the lack of emotional safety and the consequent psychosomatic illnesses, infidelities, deceptions, disturbances in their children, and general misery. Here are some of the reasons for the deadlock:

- The one who would like to divorce feels that doing so would be an admission of failure. Or the other partner may try to prevent the separation in order to avoid the suggestion that the spouse left behind is inferior. These couples remain together not out of love but out of hate. As one woman put it, "I'd leave the philandering bastard in a flash but I'll be damned if I am going to give him the opportunity to come out of this a wounded hero."

- Each partner may want the other to assume the responsibility and guilt for the breakup. Neither may want to play "bad guy" or "home wrecker" in front of the children, so they stick together in order not to let the other have the advantage. Little thought is given to what impact such an agreement has on the children.

- One or both may be too afraid of loneliness. Most people abhor loneliness, and some are so terrified that being left alone makes them feel like abandoned orphans. They married to avoid being alone or to be "rescued" from their parents; and once coupled, they could not tolerate being alone for more than a few hours. (This is like having a fear of the dark, except it operates around the clock.) They have ended up lonelier than before, and to the loneliness is added bitterness. Yet they continue together, quietly destroying each other, because of fear of being apart and alone. They lack courage.

Aside from the psychological reasons for avoiding a divorce, there are practical factors that couples offer for continuing the relationship.

Primary among these is financial circumstances. For middle-income families, the expense of two households (not to mention legal fees) presents a formidable barrier to divorce. Ultimately, the financial hardship, and the psychological needs discussed above, must be weighed against a living arrangement that slowly eats away at integrity and well-being.

FINDING A THERAPIST YOU CAN TRUST

Better and Worse

Barbara and Mark were married for twelve years and had two sons. During the last year, Barbara had been involved with another man. She didn't know whether to leave her husband or to break up the affair and try to work on improving their marriage. She decided to work on her marriage and suggested to Mark that they go for couple therapy. Mark was bitter and complained that therapy would be a waste of money: "I'm not crazy. You'd better straighten yourself out or leave. I'm staying in this house; I'm not leaving my children just because you've had a change of heart."

Barbara wasn't about to give up her home or children. She continued her plea for a neutral third party until Mark reluctantly agreed to give therapy a try. Barbara and Mark give an account of their experience; Mark relates:

At the time Barbara suggested therapy, I was enraged. I'm a decent guy. I try to do the right thing. This is what I get in return? I thought, "Goddamn it, I don't deserve this!" Besides being angry as hell, I was embarrassed. Going to a stranger and telling him that when I roll over toward my wife in bed I feel her tense up isn't my ideal way to spend an evening!

On top of all this, I felt I was living out a prophecy. My father died when I was very young, and my mother remarried and divorced twice. I've always had the nagging suspicion that having grown up in a broken home, I was destined to end up in the same circumstance. This angered me also. I felt I never stood a chance. I was also angered about the possibility of losing my children.

As a child, I knew what it was to lose a parent. I didn't want what happened to me to be repeated with my children. All in all, I was one angry guy. And all my anger was pent up. Once in a while, I would blow off at Barbara but usually I carried it around. I was like a bomb ready to explode. For the first time in my life, the thought of suicide occurred to me.

During that first session, I was beside myself. I had this feeling of inevitability. I felt Barbara was going to leave and that nothing would stop her. I felt the way people must feel when they're about to be executed. I felt helpless and empty. I remember that when the therapist mentioned that he understood I was in pain, I practically jumped on him. "Psychologist or not," I yelled, "you can't know what I'm going through unless it happened to you!"

He wasn't defensive about that. He said, "You're right. I can't experience your pain, but I sense it; I also hear it and I want you to know that." He said that in a way that told me he really meant it. I believed him, and it relieved me because I didn't feel I had to work at convincing him how bad I felt. I began to cry.

Barbara has this to say:

My choice was either to leave or to find a way of satisfying myself within the marriage. I knew I was driving Mark up the wall. He was starting to drink too much and he wasn't sleeping well at all. He was doing everything to contain himself. I married when I was eighteen— straight out of high school. My father was very strict, and I saw Mark as an escape. Probably lots of people have done the same.

Now I was going through a reevaluation. I really didn't see why I wasn't happy in my marriage. Why couldn't I get as much from Mark as I got from this other guy? I knew the only way I was going to work this out was with a therapist.

One of the early things the therapist said to us was, "I'm not in the marriage-saving business. I don't regard marriage as sacred. I regard personal happiness as primary. If the two of you can learn to contribute to each other's happiness, that's terrific. If you detract and you are either unwilling or unable to correct this, then it's up to you to decide where to go from there."

I felt a little taken back by his statement. He seemed to be implying we would have to make a lot of our own decisions about things. I guess I was expecting him to tell us what to do. I had secretly hoped he would give me "permission" to leave. I remember asking him what he thought about me leaving. He wouldn't say, "Yes, go," or "No, stay." Instead, he helped me look at the consequences of staying and leaving. It was still up to me. I knew that in the final analysis, I would have to decide, but I was aching for someone to take me off the hook.

MARK: *During the first few sessions, I had to deal with my anger. Barbara is very even tempered. I am angered easily. This was the case even before our difficulties. In therapy, I was encouraged to be more expressive and this felt good. I began to say a lot of things to Barbara that I hadn't said before. But things between us got worse. I said to the therapist, "You suggested I communicate more, really express what I'm feeling, and when I do express what I'm feeling, what do I get back? Shit!" I was getting just what I got as a child. When I opened my mouth, I got a slap. The therapist encouraged both of us not to give up. He reminded us that pain is not a signal to run.*

BARBARA: *After five months of therapy, we began to see some real changes in our relationship. The biggest thing that happened was we began to appreciate each other as individuals—adult individuals. We had been so busy catering to our view of each other's weaknesses, so preoccupied with taking care of the other person that we were both suffocating. It was a tremendous relief not to have to take care of the other but to trust in our ability to stand on our own. This was liberating for both of us. In therapy, we both began to appreciate—if not always like—each other's honest thoughts and feelings. We didn't feel we had to be overly careful about hurting each other or causing one of us to fall apart. We began to believe in each other's strength.*

MARK: *Finally after several more months, we made a joint decision to terminate therapy. We wanted to do things on our own. It's not that all our problems went away. There wasn't anything magical like that. We just began to feel more like struggling with them without any extra help. I guess we had come to a point where we felt we understood and appreciated each other. We felt we could live our lives and be fulfilled even without each other. Also, for the first time in years, we were genuinely cooperative and positive with each other. We learned to compromise to our mutual benefit. Our relationship took a mature turn. We became more desirous of each other and truly enjoyed each other's company.*

In this successful marital therapy experience, Barbara and Mark were helped in several ways, some of which may not be evident from their brief description. They were assisted to:

- develop clear communication so that the message sent is the message received;
- identify the behavioral patterns and attitudes that were impairing their relationship;
- take responsibility for their part of the marital disruption rather than blame the other;
- practice techniques designed to increase cooperative and trust-promoting behavioral patterns and to decrease negative, trust-eroding patterns; and
- develop the ability to negotiate and create workable compromises.

These are the critical areas of intervention. To the extent that a breakdown occurs in one or more of these areas, relationship distress is likely to increase. A couple seeking assistance from a competent therapist can expect help in each of these areas.

Unfortunately, as another couple, Carl and Virginia, were to learn, therapy can also be a negative experience. Unless therapy is approached skillfully, the couple's dissatisfactions and destructive patterns may be escalated rather than diminished. Carl explained:

We had been having difficulty in our marriage for some years. We really didn't have a partnership. Virginia had the kids to mind, no job, few friends. I was busy all day in a demanding job, trying to rise through the ranks. I would come home after being gone for nine or ten hours and just drop in front of the tube. We lived in separate worlds. Virginia always felt that I was too dominant and that she had to subjugate her personality to mine. She was probably right.

Then there was the sexual problem. We were married at eighteen, and in the beginning of our marriage, I was very unsure of myself sexually. I lacked experience. I was uptight about performing. I had a very strict Catholic upbringing; my Catholic school teachers and my parents seemed very down on sex—"This is a thing you don't do." I remember the first time I masturbated, when I was about fifteen, in confession, I was chastised. Psychologically, that was pretty effective. I felt guilty as hell for a year after that if I so much as thought about masturbating.

Virginia is the one who called Jack for an appointment. He was recommended by a friend. We were both pretty taken aback by Jack's manner and appearance in that first session. He was a big man, with a very large bald head, and he was sitting in the middle of his living-room office in a yoga-like position. He was very informal and almost insisted we call him by his first name immediately.

During that initial session, he encouraged us to accuse each other. I thought that one of the sanest things we had going was that we weren't into pointing to each other and complaining "You're to blame." Jack said that wasn't how we really felt. "What you really need," he insisted, "is to go through an emotional upheaval." He made the point that I especially needed this because I was the one creating the problem.

In our second session, Jack said he had been thinking about our prior discussion and he had come up with a possible solution. "I'm not going to tell you how to run your life" he started, "but I think you both need a broader sexual experience. Have this within your marriage," he continued. "Maintain your marriage and have coexisting outside relationships. This will test your commitment to each other. If you are really for each other, you can share this experience and it will strengthen the relationship."

My first reaction to Jack's statement was shock—and fear. He picked up on this and convinced me I needed this experience if I was ever going to relate satisfactorily to a woman. He said this experience

*would provide a definition of the real me. I would find myself.
Virginia needed less convincing. She admitted that she had some
curiosity about outside sexual experiences, which, I thought, was only
natural since her experiences with me were not satisfactory. So we listened to Jack and agreed that maybe he was right about the open-
marriage thing. That ended our second session.*

*It turned out that the guy who recommended Jack—my friend—
was the guy Virginia wound up in bed with. She told me about it one
night in intimate detail just as Jack had suggested: "Share the experience." I was devastated. I don't remember ever being so uncomfortable.
God, it was a painful experience. Now I was ready for blaming! But
who could I blame? I had agreed to this insanity.*

*For the first time in my life, I became impotent. Two months later,
out of sheer desperation, I called Jack for another appointment. This
time just for me—to discuss the impotence.*

*He was very casual about it. He asked how long I had been impo-
tent. I told him for over two months. His reply was, "Don't sweat it,
you'll get over it. It's natural for these things to occur." He started telling
me about his own experience with impotence but I interrupted him. His
casual, offhand, "Hey, just lean back and enjoy the trip" manner was
no consolation. I felt psychologically and sexually powerless.*

*I left the office before the end of the session. I didn't pay him or even
say anything. I just got up and walked out. That was the last I saw of
him. I never heard from him again. The next day I moved out of the
house and took a small apartment. The divorce came through three
months later.*

There are several points to be made regarding Carl and Virginia's
brief "therapy" experience:

- It is important in a prior telephone call or initial session to
  obtain information regarding the therapist's credentials and
  point of view.
- Beware of the therapist who imposes personal biases (e.g.,
  pushes open sexual involvement). This does not mean that
  therapists are not to have personal beliefs or that they are not to
  be expressed, only that they be honestly labeled as biases and
  not imposed.

- Therapists who view their role consistently as a judicial one in which they sift the evidence presented and eventually make pronouncements are, at best, inexperienced. This approach tends to be very damaging because the spouses are likely to devote their energy and ingenuity to digging up "evidence" against each other. The results? An escalation of bad feelings, and an increased schism, until the therapy and the relationship break down altogether.
- Therapists who side with one partner on an overall basis ("you're the problem") rather than as a temporary therapeutic maneuver or on a particular issue, reinforce the false idea that couple problems feature a victim or a villain. Under the pressure of gender liberation, some male therapists lean over backwards to side with the female partner in order to "prove" fairness.
- Accusing each other and blaming the relationship disturbance on each other is decidedly counterproductive. Bitter quarreling over pointless issues, particularly if it goes on session after session and is encouraged by the therapist, is not a sign of an "intense emotional upheaval" but of an incompetent therapist.

Danger Signals

How does a couple know if therapy is warranted? Relationship distress may range from overt anger to avoidance, which is underground dissatisfaction. The most obvious "red flags" indicating that a couple may have a trust problem and should consider getting the assistance of a professional third party are these:

- Frequent arguments without resolution in which one or both partners are left with hurt feelings or burning resentment. Emphasis would wisely be placed on those touchy issues involving trustworthiness. Sometimes the conflict takes the form of consistent arguments over what appear to be insignificant issues. Constant arguments about reliability—for example, showing up late or not keeping everyday agreements—may indicate an underlying trust problem.

- Feelings of being mistrusted for real or imagined reasons, or being suspicious of your partner ("How does she *really* spend her days off? She's always so evasive when I try pinning her down.").
- Frequent avoidance of each other. Often an underlying trust problem results in withdrawal. People living together can avoid each other in numerous ways. Sometimes a couple manages to have other people around all the time—frequent house guests, friends for dinner, friends to share vacations, friends to spend weekends with—hardly ever giving themselves an opportunity to be alone. (These are usually the couples whose divorce shocks their friends who thought they were "wonderfully happy together.") Television is another convenient barrier. Overwork or overinvolvement in avocational pursuits can also be a danger signal.
- Overdependence on the part of one or both partners. This can be expressed by constant "checking" on each other, not feeling comfortable and worthwhile without a mate's companionship, resentment of a mate's independent interests, living for the other's achievements, and being overly sensitive to the other's criticism.
- Sexual dissatisfaction. This includes lack of attraction, inability to "let go" in bed, a lack of affection, warmth, and mutual sexual pleasuring. Also significant are outside sexual relationships.

These are some of the more common danger signals; variations are infinite in number. When should you seek help?

Not after a short-lived, shallow dip in domestic satisfaction. A day's arguing over the children, a few days of melancholy or self-pity, a siege of jealousy—these are not necessarily signals of trouble. They are more probably results of the normal strain of living in a difficult world. The key to watch for is repetition, a continued feeling of resentment, boredom, lovelessness, hurt, and sexual dissatisfaction.

What *Not* to Expect

When we are little children and we fall, bruising our knee, Mommy or Daddy kisses the injury and makes it all better. They do magic. When we get sick and the doctor comes, administers some pills, and cures our ailment, the doctor does magic. When we are grownup and have marital problems, we go to another type of doctor, the marriage doctor, expecting that he or she will make the marriage all better, like magic. Unfortunately, therapy doesn't work that way. There are no magic pills, no magic wands to wave.

A passive stance—"Therapy will make us all better"—is an attitude that guarantees failure. This is probably the most common unrealistic expectation that couples bring to therapy. It resembles the erroneous attitude that a relationship will prosper by itself: "Now that we're married, the relationship will grow." Most of us know that the latter notion is false, but it is a tempting trap. In actuality, a marriage works because the marital partners work at it. This applies equally to therapy.

Other expectations that increase the likelihood of *dissatisfaction* with therapy are:

- "Marital therapy is designed to keep the marriage together." This is not true. Therapy is supposed to help couples clarify their own needs, wishes, and feelings. It also helps the partners identify in their spouses those traits that meet their needs and those that do not. The attitude of a professional is likely to be: "My job is to help these people stay together more compatibly and productively—or to help them separate as amiably as possible. Since this is not my marriage, it is not within my province to decide which of these two courses to take."

- "The marital therapist, being an intelligent individual, will see my side of things and straighten out my spouse, who is really the problem." Very often this is the hidden agenda. However, if the therapist takes sides, the therapy may seem to go well for the "righteous mate" but the marriage is most likely to deteriorate. A more productive attitude involves shared responsibility for dissatisfaction.

- "I should feel comfortable throughout therapy." It is not comfortable to change old habits. Consequently, the therapeutic process is likely to be painful at times. Serenity is hard to maintain while sensitive issues are being brought to awareness and confronted as never before. Also, the progress of the partners is likely to be uneven; when one opens up, the other may rebuff him or her. Result: hurt and angry feelings. Sensitive therapists support the rebuffed partner, encouraging that person not to give up while helping the other to be more responsive. But still it hurts. Discomfort in therapy is unavoidable; and its total absence is a sign that the process is merely superficial.

- "If we are sincere and work hard, things will improve immediately." Change is not easy and it is not instant. A relationship may even worsen before it gets better. Dissatisfaction, hurt feelings, anger, and misunderstanding are not quickly cleared up. Yet people tend, after a few sessions, to conclude things are all better. Frequently, this is a premature decision based on an avoidance of further exploration of "hot" issues.
- "We can always go into therapy in the future; things aren't that bad now." One of the biggest frustrations of marital therapists is that couples hesitate to seek help until the situation is desperate. Then they come to the therapist and expect to be bailed out. By this time, the relationship may have been severely damaged and the willingness to work at it almost exhausted. But little can be done to help marriages that are extremely disturbed. They generally break up in the end, and the partners unfairly ridicule the skills of the therapist when, in fact, a Solomon couldn't have prevented the breakup. If these same couples had begun therapy earlier, before things became intolerable and all caring stopped, they could have been spared years of marital suffering and misery.

Types of Marital Therapists

Successful therapy relationships depend less on the therapist's professional title than on training, experience, and personal qualities. Yet knowing something about the classes of therapists makes for a more informed choice. The three major classes of mental health practitioners are psychiatrists, psychologists, and social workers. Professionally trained marital therapists, counselors, and nurse practitioners also offer treatment services to the public. A brief discussion of each follows.

Psychiatrists

Psychiatrists are physicians who have completed medical training and have obtained a medical degree (M.D.). In some states, a psychiatrist need not have completed specialized training beyond the medical degree to practice psychiatry. That is, physicians with no special training in human behavior can call themselves a psychiatrist or marital therapist with no approval necessary from a public accrediting body. Rather than formal training in the psychology of marital problems or supervised experience in helping persons solve their most pressing problems, psychiatrists are mainly schooled in handling patients administratively—with drugs and hospitalization—and giving psychological first aid.

Psychiatrists who have had advanced training, particularly those who have completed the requirements of the American Board of Psychiatry, have usually spent three years in psychiatric residence beyond the four years in medical school and a general (medical) internship. A good part of the residency may have been at a large mental institution such as a city or state hospital. In this setting, the psychiatrist probably dealt with severely disturbed persons, such as schizophrenics or chronic alcoholics.

Some of the training period, usually about six months, is spent working with neurological problems (disorders caused by diseases of the brain or nerves). Some time is frequently devoted to work in an outpatient clinic, where the physician sees a variety of patients with a variety of problems.

A few psychiatrists doing marital therapy rely heavily on medical methods, especially the administration of psychoactive drugs. This is certainly not the rule, but it is most common among those with insufficient advanced training in marital therapy. Such a psychiatrist is likely to prescribe drugs in an effort to "give the patients something." Unfortunately, problems of living are rarely solved by drugs.

How can you ascertain psychiatrists' methods of practice? Asking someone who has seen them in therapy may be helpful. Psychiatrists may briefly discuss their orientation in a telephone conversation.

If nothing else is known except that a psychiatrist is qualified (with an M.D. and has certification from the American Board of Psychiatry), an initial consultation is wise. The couple should arrange to meet the therapist together and jointly ask about methods and point of view.

Asking pointed questions of the therapist as to training, experience, and attitudes may seem rude or unnecessary, but remember that therapy is an important and expensive venture whose success depends, in part, upon the choice of the proper therapist. Couples may have to visit two or three different psychiatrists before finding one with whom they both feel comfortable and confident.

Psychologists

A professional psychologist holds a doctoral degree (Ph.D., Ed.D., or Psy.D.) from an accredited university or professional school in a program that is mainly psychological in content. The doctor's degree takes five years beyond the four-year college degree to complete. This includes a one-year supervised internship.

All states have laws regulating the practices of psychologists. To practice marital therapy, appropriate registration, certification, or licensing is required. Most states forbid anyone else to represent to the public any title or description of services for a fee with the words, "psychology," "psychological," or "psychologist." Lacking a medical degree, psychologists are not permitted to prescribe drugs. (Psychologists may refer patients to a medical doctor for a drug prescription.)

Psychologists are concerned with the dynamics of personality and behavior, but their training varies considerably. As a group, psychologists have far more training in principles of human behavior than do psychiatrists or social workers. Yet not all have had specialized training in applying their knowledge to marital disturbances. (Some have a strong background in experimental psychology, testing theories of behavior. Others focus on industrial psychology or personnel management.) Psychologists in the private (or agency) practice of marital therapy usually have a background in the relevant specialties of clinical or counseling psychology, but it is wise to ask practitioners about their specific experience.

Social Workers

The minimum standard for a professional social worker is a master's degree in social work (M.S.W.), earned by the completion of a rigorous two-year program of graduate study in an accredited school of social work. This training includes a two-year supervised intern-

ship, working two or three days a week in an agency that offers counseling services, such as a psychiatric clinic, a hospital, a probation
department, a welfare department, or a family counseling clinic.
Usually, individuals accepted into a graduate school of social work
have an undergraduate degree (B.S. or B.A.) in one of the social or
behavioral sciences.

Most states license or certify the practice of social work. The
National Academy of Social Work provides national board certification;
it also strives to enforce professional standards together with strong
local and state social work organizations.

A couple desiring marital therapy would normally apply for this service at a family counseling service where the professional degree is
required for employment. (A few agencies, such as departments of
county welfare, use the term "social worker" for individuals without the
M.S.W. degree.) As you seek a private practitioner, confirm that the
person has earned a master's degree in social work from an accredited
institution.

Ask the social worker questions regarding professional experience.
One pertinent question is, "Have you had supervised experience in
marital therapy?" Typically, social work students are offered a general
program during their two years of training. This includes group work,
individual casework, and community organization. A few social work
schools provide for specialization in one of these areas. Thus, a student
interested in training in marital and family therapy may be assigned a
family counseling agency for internship. Others may obtain specialized
training after obtaining the graduate degree. With appropriate training,
social workers are as qualified to do marital therapy as psychiatrists and
psychologists trained in this area.

Marital Therapists and Others

"Marital therapist" is a general term that can include social workers,
psychologists, psychiatrists, pastoral counselors—and just about any
individual who wants to use the term, credentialed or not. The title is
not restricted. However, to belong to the American Association of
Marriage and Family Therapy (AAMFT), the practitioner must have a
master's degree in marriage and family therapy or a related field, and
two years' postgraduate supervised clinical training.

In addition, nurse practitioners may do marital therapy. If so, they have a master's degree or its equivalent in nursing, with a specialization in psychiatric nursing.

Professional counselors and pastoral counselors are also licensed in many states. They must have at least a master's degree and postgraduate supervised experience.

The Search

Competent professional intervention has improved many ailing marriages; therapists have helped couples to reconsider their relationship and move in more constructive directions. You increase your chances of reaping the very real benefits of therapy if you can evaluate a therapist with some sophistication. The following words of caution are offered in that spirit.

Finding a satisfactory therapist is often difficult. Recommendations made by friends, physicians, and lawyers can be useful; yet a therapist who is quite helpful to one couple may not be helpful at all to another. Reputation is often a clue, but sometimes the popular therapist is the one who pleases—rather than effectively intervenes. Some therapists without academic credentials are very talented. However, in a field where incompetence and fraud are not uncommon, it is safer to choose a therapist with reputable training and experience.

Unfortunately, professional qualifications do not tell whether the preparation was minimal, uninspired, or top quality. Further, since all forms of therapy are a mixture of art and science, the personality of the therapist is also important. A marital therapist may be a happily married man or woman who accepts life, marriage, and people, or a dour individual whose marriage is sterile and who approaches marital problems with a "what can you expect" attitude.

Sometimes marital therapists are very directive in their approach, to the point of becoming impatient or irritated if their clients fail to follow their suggestions immediately. Others are so timidly nondirective that their clients feel they are providing the therapist with an interesting hour of conversation and gaining nothing in return. Occasionally a practitioner will have a moralistic attitude toward sex, divorce, or life itself that is conveyed in judgmental proclamations about "right and wrong." Or, the therapist may have an irresponsible, "liberated," egotistical attitude that causes confusion and uncertainty.

Even the best therapist with the best training is bound to have bad days. And however well intentioned, a therapist's interventions cannot always be correct. The mark of a professional is not perfection; it is a willingness to admit mistakes and learn from them.

It's Your Call

Whenever we go to a doctor, a lawyer—anybody in authority—the child in us is apt to come out. We don't question; we don't trust our own judgment. But in making a decision about a therapist, one's own judgment is critical. People often depend on a therapist to help with serious issues; a poor choice can have far-reaching consequences.

After credentials, personal qualities, and reputation have been considered, the final decision as to compatibility rests on the couple's shoulders. The most effective way of deciding is to get referrals from several sources—professional associations, friends, and other professionals—and shop around. Admittedly, shopping can be expensive because a few visits to a therapist may be needed before a reasonable judgment can be made. On the other hand, the first therapist chosen may prove to be quite suitable.

To aid in making a realistic appraisal of the therapist, a list of seventeen questions (adapted from Lazarus and Fay's book, *I Can If I Want To*) follows.

EVALUATING A THERAPIST

Responses are scored from 0 to 4; 0 equals never or not at all; 1, slightly or occasionally; 2, sometimes or moderately; 3, a great deal or most of the time; and 4, markedly or all of the time.

Circle the number that best reflects your feelings and observations and then obtain a total score.

	ALMOST NEVER TRUE	RARELY TRUE	OCCASIONALLY TRUE	FREQUENTLY TRUE	ALMOST ALWAYS TRUE
1. I feel comfortable with the therapist.	0	1	2	3	4
2. The therapist seems to be comfortable with me.	0	1	2	3	4
3. The therapist is casual and informal rather than stiff and formal.	0	1	2	3	4
4. The therapist does not treat me as if I'm sick, defective, and about to fall apart.	0	1	2	3	4
5. The therapist is flexible and open to new ideas rather than pursuing a point of view.	0	1	2	3	4
6. The therapist has a good sense of humor and a pleasant disposition.	0	1	2	3	4
7. The therapist is willing to tell me how he/she feels about me.	0	1	2	3	4
8. The therapist admits limitations and does not pretend to know everything.	0	1	2	3	4

	ALMOST NEVER TRUE	RARELY TRUE	OCCASIONALLY TRUE	FREQUENTLY TRUE	ALMOST ALWAYS TRUE
9. The therapist is very willing to acknowledge being wrong and apologizes for making errors or for being inconsiderate, instead of justifying this kind of behavior.	0	1	2	3	4
10. The therapist answers direct questions rather than simply asking me what I think.	0	1	2	3	4
11. The therapist reveals things about herself/himself either sponta- neously or in response to my inquiries (but not by bragging and talking incessantly and irrelevantly).	0	1	2	3	4
12. The therapist encourages the feeling that I am as good as he/she is.	0	1	2	3	4

	ALMOST NEVER TRUE	RARELY TRUE	OCCASIONALLY TRUE	FREQUENTLY TRUE	ALMOST ALWAYS TRUE
13. The therapist acts as if he/she is my consultant rather than the manager of my life.	0	1	2	3	4
14. The therapist encourages differences of opinion rather than telling me that I am resisting if I disagree with him/her.	0	1	2	3	4
15. The therapist is interested in seeing people who share my life (or at least is willing to do so); this would include the significant people in my environment.	0	1	2	3	4
16. The things the therapist says make sense to me.	0	1	2	3	4
17. In general, my contacts with the therapist lead to my feeling more hopeful and to better accepting myself.	0	1	2	3	4

A perfect score on this instrument (68) is most unlikely.
A rating above the mid-forties is an indication of a sound
choice, a rating between 35 and 40 is borderline, and a score
below that is indicative of a poor choice.

In marital therapy, the therapist chosen must be acceptable to both partners. A big difference in regard would likely add strain to an already burdened relationship. As mentioned earlier, it may take several sessions before a reasonable judgment can be made. But sometimes a good match is obvious.

Cost and Length of Therapy

One of the most important considerations for many couples is the cost of therapy. The range is very broad, and is complicated by managed care companies that set fees for therapists on their panel. The advantage of a therapist who is not part of managed care is increased confidentiality and continuity of' care, without the dictates of an anonymous case manager who would like nothing better than to have treatment terminate.

Community agencies and family institutes, both public and private, generally have lower fee schedules and may even have a sliding scale based on income. Listings of these agencies are available in the reference section of a public library or through a local mental health association. Here are several suggestions regarding fees:

- It is wise not to become involved with a therapist whose fees you will not be able to afford on a weekly basis for at least several months.
- When there is legitimate financial reason, it is not "impolite" to ask if a therapist will reduce the fee. Some will, others won't. Most won't offer unless asked.
- Do not regard the size of a fee as a reflection of ability. There is no relationship. Some competent therapists have a relatively low fee schedule; others bordering on incompetence are exorbitant.

- Whatever the fee, it is not unusual to feel resentful. Payment for an intangible service is hard to accept. Most payments we make result in something that can be driven, eaten, worn, or shown off. Therapy provides none of these!

Just as fee schedules vary, so do recommendations concerning the frequency with which couples need to see the therapist and the length of time the therapy takes. In many instances, it will be suggested that therapy occur once a week jointly, for forty-five to sixty minutes. Sometimes therapists also suggest seeing one or both partners individually. If the marital difficulties are quite serious, therapy is likely to continue for one or two years. As progress is made, the frequency of sessions will likely be decreased. Sometimes, although the problems appear severe at first glance, progress is established in a relatively short time and methods for continuing progress without therapy are suggested.

Regardless of the duration of therapy, progress rarely proceeds in a neat forward direction. Rather, periods of stagnation, or even backsliding, are to be expected. (Freud termed these reverses "negative therapeutic reactions" and ascribed them to an unconscious sense of guilt that bars improvement. However, Freud's explanation seems ill-suited to the dynamics of many people.) Indeed, going nowhere and "two steps back" are part of even the most successful therapy experiences. If both partners want to work out their trust issues, the likelihood they will succeed, despite obstacles, is very favorable.

BIBLIOGRAPHY

Barker, R. L. *The Green-Eyed Marriage.* New York: Free Press, 1987.

Berne, Eric. *Games People Play: The Psychology of Human Relationships.* New York: Grove Press, 1964.

Bowlby, John. *A Secure Base.* New York: Basic Books, 1990.

Broderick, Carlton B. "Should a Husband or Wife Confess Infidelity?" *Medical Aspects of Human Sexuality* 5 (1970): 9–13.

Cappon, Daniel. "The Anatomy of Intuition." *Psychology Today* 26, No. 3 (May–June, 1993): 40–48.

Cozby, P. W. "Self Disclosure: A Literature Review." *Psychological Bulletin* (1973): 79, 73–91.

Deutsch, Helene. *Confrontations with Myself.* New York: W. W. Norton & Co., 1973.

Erikson, Erik H. *Identity, Youth and Crisis.* New York: W. W. Norton & Co., 1968.

Farber, Leslie H. *Lying, Despair, Jealousy, Envy, Sex, Suicide, Drugs, and the Good Life.* New York: Basic Books, 1976.

Fisher, Milton. *Intuition: How to Use It in Your Life.* Connecticut: Wildcat Publishing Co., 1981.

Gilligan, Carol. *In a Different Voice: Psychological Theory and Women's Development.* Cambridge, Mass.: Harvard University Press, 1993.

Goffman, Erving. *The Presentation of Self in Everyday Life.* New York: Doubleday, 1959.

Gottman, J., C. Notarius, et. al. *A Couple's Guide to Communication.* Champaign, IL: Research Press, 1976.

Graham, Gini. *The Empowered Mind: How to Harness the Creative Force Within You.* New Jersey: Prentice Hall, 1993.

Graham, Gini. *Mind Power: Picture Your Way to Success in Business.* New Jersey: Prentice Hall, 1987.

Greer, Jane. *How Could You Do This to Me?* New York: Doubleday, 1997.

Harlow, Harry F., and M. Harlow. "Learning to Love." *American Scientist* 54, no. 3 (1966): 190–201.

Kelly, George. *The Psychology of Personal Constructs.* New York: W. W. Norton & Co., 1955.

Lazarus, Arnold, and Allen Fay. *I Can If I Want To.* New York: William Morrow and Co., 1975.

Lederer, William J., and Don D. Jackson. *The Mirages of Marriage.* New York: W. W. Norton & Co., 1968.

Llewellyn, Charles E. "Should a Husband or Wife Confess Infidelity?" *Medical Aspects of Human Sexuality* 5 (1970): 14–15.

Maslow, Abraham. *Toward a Psychology of Being.* Princeton, NJ: D. Van Nostrand, 1968.

Nadel, Laurie, Judy Haims, and Robert Stempson. *Sixth Sense.* New York: Avon Books, 1992.

Pike, James A. *You and the New Morality.* New York: Harper & Row, 1967.

Pines, Ayala M. *Romantic Jealousy.* New York: Routledge, 1998.

Smith, Peter. *The Philosophy of Mind.* London: Cambridge University Press, 1987.

Vaihinger, Hans. *The Philosophy of As-If.* Translated by C. K. Ogden. New York: Charles Scribner's Sons, 1924.

Vaughan, Diane. *Uncoupling: Turning Points in Intimate Relationships.* New York: Oxford University Press, 1986.

Wallerstein, Judith, and Sandra Blakeslee. *Second Chances: Men, Women and Children a Decade After Divorce.* New York: Houghton Mifflin Co., 1996.

Winn, Harold. "Should a Husband or Wife Confess Infidelity?"
  Medical Aspects of Human Sexuality 5 (1970): 8.
Winnicott, D. W. *The Family and Individual Development.* New York:
  Basic Books, 1965.

INDEX

ABOUT THE AUTHOR

Joel D. Block, Ph.D., is a clinical psychologist practicing couple and individual psychotherapy on Long Island, NY. A diplomate of the American Board of Professional Psychology, Dr. Block is a supervisor at the Human Sexuality Center of Long Island Jewish Medical Center and an assistant clinical professor at the Einstein College of Medicine. He is the author of numerous magazine articles and nine books including *Sex Over 50, Secrets of Better Sex, Friendship, Lasting Love, To Marry Again,* and *The Other Man, the Other Woman.* Dr. Block lives and practices in Huntington, NY.